The Spiritual Gems

of Judaism & Sikhism

A comparative study of the oldest

to the youngest religion

Harsimran Singh, Ph.D.

ੴ

Dedicated to Almighty God

in gratitude for his best gift:

The gift of my lovely children

Rohan, Punit, Gunit & Pavit.

Table Of Contents

Section 3 THE OPPOSING FORCES

Section 4 CAUTION

Preface

After I wrote the book, *Power of Prayer & 10 World Religions,* it was amazing to find tremendous similarities between Judaism and Sikhism.

The similarities between the world's oldest religion and the youngest religion prompted me to write this book.

It is also amazing to see that the followers of both religions have tremendous social, cultural and economic similarities.

Praying for the universal peace and understanding for the followers of all religions of the world.

Dr. Harsimran Singh

Acknowledgments

I am thankful to Gurdip Singh from Baramulla, Kashmir, India for his help in research of my writings on Sikhism.

I am also thankful to Russ Shulkes. His extreme knowledge of Judaism was a great help to me. It would have been very difficult for me to present my book in this form without his active, sincere and intellectual help. He has already earned three masters degrees and is now pursuing his Ph.D.

<u>JEWISH PRAYER</u>

God, hear my song;

listen to my prayer.

With a faint heart,

from the ends of the land, I call to You;

lead me with the rock that is higher than I.

For You have been a refuge to me;

a tower of might against the enemy.

I shall dwell in Your tent forever;

I shall take refuge in the shelter of Your wings, forever.

Psalms 61: 2-5

SYMBOL OF JUDAISM

The Star of David

Also known as 'The Magen David', the six-pointed star is the symbol most commonly associated with Judaism today. The star is supposed to be the shape of King David's shield.

Basic Jewish Beliefs

Maimonides, the famous 13th century philosopher and jurist, listed thirteen "fundamentals of faith" in one of his commentaries. These principles have become accepted as the hallmark of traditional Judaism. They are:

1) To know that God exists
2) God is One
3) God is non-corporeal
4) God pre-dated everything
5) Only God should be served
6) Prophecy
7) Moses was the greatest prophet
8) The Torah is from Heaven
9) The Torah has not been changed
10) God is aware of mankind's actions
11) God rewards and punishes
12) Messiah
13) Resurrection of the Dead

JUDAISM
at a glance

Judaism is the oldest of the Middle-eastern religions. It is the parent-religion of the two largest world-faiths: Christianity and Islam. It is the religion of God's chosen people: the Israelites. Abraham, originally from Ur in Babylon, founded Judaism around the 1750 B.C in the Mesopotamian lands. Their belief is that there is only One God, who is omnipresent, omnipotent, omniscient, eternal, perfect, just and gracious. He created humans in His own image. People are capable of perfecting themselves through upholding God's commandments and through embracing certain philosophical premises.

Judaism is a monotheistic faith, as are some forms of Christianity, Islam, and Sikhism. The soul, according to Judaism, is given to mankind upon his birth. But, at that point it is pure potential: a person must develop this soul in order to actualize its potential and earn its immortality in the next world.

In the Torah's opening verse, it says that the universe was created out of nothingness (*ex nihilo*). As God is perfect, it follows that, not only that He is good, but that everything the He creates it good. Hence, everything in creation is good, if we could but understand each thing's purpose.

Jews believe in heaven, a limited hell, and the devil (which is equated with man's evil inclination). Whenever one transgresses one of the Lord's commandments, he has committed a sin. Evil springs up when one forsakes the path laid out in the Torah, and blindly follows his senses, superstitions and man-made rituals. The so-called existence of evil tendencies in mankind is a test for human beings, who have been blessed with the intellect to make free will decisions. Sincerity, selflessness, prayer, repentance, following the commandments and service-to-humanity, are the essentials for attaining true peace and happiness in this world and the next.

The Prophets of ancient Israel perceived the activity of Yahweh in the history of their people. They saw that Yahweh, the 'God of the Exodus', brought the oppressed Israelites, living in bondage under the Egyptians, to freedom and a new way of life in the land of C'naan. These prophets received the Divine initiative to lead the Jewish people throughout history, until the mankind lost the ability to prophecy before the advent of Christianity.

From about 1000 B.C., Moses was succeeded by a line of Davidic kings, beginning with the founder of this line King David the son of Yishai. The Prophetic books describe the monarchy of each king in terms of if he followed God's ways (by repudiating idolatry and following the commandments) or not. Sometime during this period, the belief that a king from the Davidic line would rise up to lead the Jewish people to freedom and restore Israel to its former pre-eminent position arose. He would liberate the Jewish people from non-Jewish rulership: this man is called the Messiah or Christ.

The Tanakh, especially the Torah (first five books of the Tanakh), are considered the word of God. Moses, the prophet who wrote these five books, was considered as a conduit for the Divine message. The Talmud (a commentary on the Oral Law written in the 6th century by Babylonian rabbis) contains all the rules and theology which traditional follow. In medieval times, rabbis like Maimonides and Rashi commented on these writings and collected them into law codes. Nonetheless, in today's times, there are four branches of Judaism: Orthodox (or traditional), Conservative, Reform and Reconstructionist.

For Orthodox Jews, God is the personal, all-powerful, eternal and compassionate God that freed the Hebrews from bondage 3,200 years ago. Obviously, they reject the notion of the Holy Trinity of Christianity and that Mohammed was a prophet. Not only was Jesus not the Messiah, but he was not even a respected rabbi by the majority of the Jews in the 1st century.

Traditional Jews believe that prayer, repentance, and obeying the God given commandments are essential for attaining Salvation. The obedient shall be honored in Heaven and shall live there forever with God, while the unrighteous shall be condemned to excision.

The Torah

When Jews use the word Torah, or Bible, it can have one of three meanings. In its most restricted and widely used sense, it is a synonym for the five books of Moses, encompassing the text that orthodox Jewry believe to be the direct communication between God and human divines.

The Torah found in the arch of every synagogue is a copy of these five holy books, painstakingly handwritten on parchment by a professional scribe, which together are called the Pentateuch, coming from the root word 'penta' meaning five.

The Jewish people believe that only the Bible is holy and from God, while Christians believe that the Old Testament was superseded by the New Testament, even though both works are holy. They believe that the special covenant between God and the Jewish people was taken away and given to the new Israel of the Church. In other words, Christians are the new Jews.

When one uses the word 'Torah,' he may be referring to the later books of the Prophets appended to the five books of Moses. Together, these form what is referred to by the Jews as the Bible. In this larger version of the Bible, there are 24 books in all. In general, though, these 24 books are called the Tanakh. Tanakh is an acronym for Torah, Nevi'im (Prophets), Ketuvim (Writings).

The third meaning of Torah is based on its literal definition. Torah is a teaching, a doctrine, a law. Any discussion of the Bible, any analysis that helps us to understand the Bible better is a teaching, and therefore qualifies to be called Torah.

The deeper root meaning of Torah is that it springs from the word 'yarah' which means "to shoot" (at a target). Obviously, to shoot at something, an arrow must be directed in that direction. So, by inference we can safely say that Torah means "correct direction". Torah advises and recommends the right path to tread.

The five books of the Torah are:

- 'Genesis,' which comes from the first of the verse chapter of the first verse of the Torah. In means: "In the beginning." This book takes us from the Creation and the beginning of history, through the Hebrew forefathers and foremothers, until the Hebrews traveled from C'naan to live with Joseph inn Egypt.

- 'Exodus' is the second book. This name is not drawn from the first word of the book, but instead from its theme: "going out" (of Egypt, of slavery and of bondage). This book contains the exodus of the Israelites from Egypt, the giving of the Torah to the Israelites at Mount Sinai and the building of the tabernacle. Also, it contains hundreds of rules in which the Israelites were to follow and base society upon.

- 'Leviticus' is the third book of the Torah. It is named after the tribe Levi who were appointed to serve in the tabernacle, and eventually in the Temple, in the stead of the firstborns. This book gives the detailed instructions of Temple service and sacrifices.

- 'Numbers' the fourth book. It contains censuses of the Israelites as well as details of their forty year stay within the Sinai desert. Also, several Israelite rebellions are chronicled.

- 'Deuteronomy,' the last book of the Pentateuch, literally meaning "the second law." This book centers around the Moses' lengthy farewell address to the Israelites right before they enter the land of C'naan, recapitulating what had happened to the Jews until then, as well as the covenant they made with God that would ensure their survival in the land of Israel.

The Biblical Heroes

Abraham

Abraham was the founder of the Jewish people. He was originally called Abram. After he became a believer in the One God, his name was changed by the Deity to make it encompass a wider meaning "father of many nations." Originally, Abram restricted his leadership to a small group, but once he came to recognize God and accept monotheism, Abraham took it upon himself to spread the word of God to all peoples of the world. He was on a mission to share the spiritual truths with the entire world, not a small limited area.

Sarah

Abraham's wife Sarah also had another name before her acceptance of the Judaism creeds. She was Sarai, meaning princess, but her name was changed to princess of God and of mankind. She worked hand in hand with Abraham proselytizing throughout the land of C'naan.

Isaac and Rebecca

Isaac, the son of Sarah and Abraham, carried forward the spiritual teachings of his parents. His name is derived from the Hebrew root for laughter, because it seemed ridiculous when an angel told Abraham, aged 100, and Sarah, aged 90, that they would be blessed with their first child. The birth of Isaac (Yitshak) proved that when God could control everything under the sun.

Isaac was an extremely righteous individual. Even though God promised that he would be Abraham's sole heir, he had such confidence in God and his father that when his father bound him to an altar, at God's behest, he stood still awaiting his Divine fait (even though Abraham, again because of Divine initiative) refrained from slaughtering his son.

Jacob

Jacob (Ya'akov) in Hebrew means: "heel". A child of Isaac and Rebecca, he was passive, introverted, and non-confrontational in his early years. He was somebody on whom people could easily "step upon" and dominate. Only later in life, he realized that he had to change to win, for God doesn't fight all the battles for us, if we are not ready and willing to work a little. In a traumatic moment when he fought an attacker, his name was changed to Israel (Yisrael), meaning "a fighter for God". Ya'akov life was fraught with sadness and troubles reminding us that even God's chosen ones do not get a free ride

Rachel

She was the love of Jacob's life. Her name comes from "the beloved." When his prospective father-in-law Laban made him work seven years, for Rachel's hand, Jacob worked happily. But, Laban was deceitful. He gave Leah, his older daughter in marriage instead claiming that was how his culture acted. So, he worked another seven years for his true love. Since bigamy wasn't banned until then, he was doubly blessed, marrying Rachel and Leah happily and fathering children with both of them as well as with both of their maidservants. In total, Jacob fathered twelve boys and one girl.

The Twelve Tribes

The next twelve heroes came in rapid succession. Jacob's twelve sons are Ruben, Simon, Levi, Judah, Issachar, Zebulan, Dan, Naftali, Gad, Asher, Joseph, and Benjamin. These are the children of Israel, each of whom eventually represented a large tribe when the Israelites left Egypt. Eventually, when ten of the tribes were exiled, only the tribes of Judah and Benjamin play a prominent role.

When the Jewish people later settled in C'naan, the Promised Land of Israel, the country was divided into twelve sections so that every tribe could have its own domain. The result was something of a confederation of autonomous states, enjoined by a treaty of sorts, maintaining a distinctive quality, while sharing common ideals and objectives, remaining unified as one nation.

Moses

Three generations after the children of Israel were born, Amrom, the grandson of Levi, married Yocheved, and they had a child named Moses. Unfortunately, as the Pharaoh took up a policy of infanticide and proclaimed that all male Jewish children should be executed upon birth. Yocheved, Moses' mother hid him for three months, but when she could hide him no longer, she devised a plan in which he could be saved. Playing on the fact that the Egyptians deemed the Nile a god, she sent him in a little ark until he was found by none other than Pharaoh's daughter. Ironically, Pharaoh's daughter paid

Yocheved to nurse the boy until he was weaned and could go love in the palace with her.

She named him Moses, because "from the water she drew him." She raised him in the very place where he would later play a prominent role for his people. Who would have known that this would be the man who would become the greatest leader in all of Jewish history?

Aaron

Aaron was the brother of Moses. Even though he was the elder, Moses was the recognized leader. Nonetheless, Aaron was a great man in his own right, and was also given a position of prominence by God. He became the High Priest in the tabernacle, and then in his line were to administer in the Temple; they were charged with overseeing all the religious duties, functions and responsibilities that go on in the Temple.

Role of Women and Family

The Bible describes God as taking the rib from man and "building" it into a woman. It uses the Hebrew word '*va'yiven*' which is related to the word for profound understanding (binah). Based on that, the Talmud concludes that God endowed women with more insight and intuitive intelligence than men.

And when the Talmud wonders why, at the time of Revelation, God told Moses to first "speak to the daughters of Israel" before addressing the men, and to ask them whether they wished to receive the Torah, the response is: "Because the way of men is to follow the opinion of women."

Woman is seen to have one more attribute in much greater measure than man. The Hebrew word for kindness, *rachamim,* has as its root *rechem,* which means womb.

The very name of God that expresses this characteristic of mercifulness and compassion appears in Hebrew with a feminine ending. God Him/Herself sometimes chooses to be more like a woman.

One of the very first directives God gave to Adam and Eve was, "Be fruitful and multiply." Jewish theologians explain that in principle, the notion of *imitatio Dei,* (imitating God) prescribes Jews to be more like God; they must create in order to continue the world God brought into being. According to normative Jewish law, Jews may not remain childless. The minimum number of children necessary to fulfill this biblical requirement is two: one boy and one girl. Of course, if a married couple tries and fails to conceive, they cannot be blamed. But, to avoid parenthood is considered a sin.

Traditions

Jewish law provides guidance to its followers from the cradle to the grave. The Jewish people have been persecuted for many ages. As such, children are their secret to survival and a viable future.

Jews often congratulate each other with the words '*mazel tov'*. The phrase is generally translated to mean 'good luck', however *mazel* refers to a constellation, one of the signs of the Zodiac. While Jews may not believe that the stars determine fate, some may believe that the stars have an influence. Mosaic floors in some of the ancient synagogues depict the signs of the Zodiac showing that this belief can be traced back thousands of years.

Jewish tradition says that when parents choose a name for a new baby, they are blessed with Divine Inspiration. Jewish children are given a Jewish name in addition to their secular one. Ashkenazic Jews of certain parts Europe do not name a child after a living person. They believe that it is too soon to see if the living person will turn out wicked in the end and that it would therefore be unfair to link a child to someone whose end is unsure. The Sephardic Jews, from Eastern European and Oriental heritage, believe in honoring a person, usually the four grandparents first, they most respect and admire during their lifetime by naming children after them.

A girl is given her Jewish name at the synagogue the next time that the Torah is read after her birth. A boy, on the other hand, receives his name on the eighth day after his birth as part of the *brit millah,* or circumcision ceremony.

Circumcision in the Bible is called a "sign of the flesh". By removing the foreskin, a Jew becomes visibly different in his very body. It is a spiritual link with God that can never be removed. The person who performs the circumcision is known as a *mohel* and the person who holds the baby, which is a great honor, is called the *sandek.* In mystic tradition, the sandek is showered with blessings from God for his role. When the circumcision is complete, all present join in a prayer of three wishes to the child: "May he grow to a life of Torah, to *chuppah* (the wedding canopy), and to good deeds."

When a male child reaches the age of 13, he becomes *Bar Mitzvah,* or a "son of the commandments'. He is called to the Torah to recite blessings or lead the congregation in prayer. On this day, a boy becomes a man because he is considered mature enough to be responsible for his actions. At this age, it is now incumbent upon him to follow all the rules of the Torah and the Rabbis.

Judaism recognizes that girls mature faster than boys and for this reason, girls receive *Bat Mitzvah* when they are 12.

In Judaism, marriage is clearly commanded in the Bible: "Therefore shall a man leave his father and his mother, and cleave unto his wife, and they shall be one flesh." (Genesis 2:24). When a wedding date is set, there is only one restriction: a wedding cannot be held on the same day as another Jewish festival. This is because Jews are told, "We must not mix one joy with another." The ceremony itself takes place under a canopy called a *chuppah*. In the first part of the ceremony, the bride circles the husband seven times, mystically demonstrating that she is entering the seven spheres of her beloved's soul. In front of witnesses, the man recites the words "You are made holy to me with this ring according to the religion of Moses and Israel." He gives her the ring, and they are married.

Probably the most commonly recognized feature of a Jewish wedding ceremony is the breaking of a glass by the groom at the conclusion. Though marriage is considered a time of supreme happiness, the breaking of the glass is to remind Jewish people that their joy cannot be complete as long as the Temple in Jerusalem remains destroyed. It reminds them that rejoicing must be tempered with remembrance of their people's catastrophes. In modern terms, it would be the equivalent of saying they must never forget the Holocaust, no matter how happy they are.

Death, in the Jewish view, is a matter of going from one room to another. Judaism teaches that God endowed humans with His essence and therefore, "the spirit returns unto God who gave it." Death is the moment of separation of the soul from the body.

Orthodox Jews are profoundly opposed to cremation. Jewish tradition demands a simple pine coffin. Burial follows so that the Biblical decree, "to dust you shall return" can be fulfilled with the body's decay in the ground. The deceased must also be buried as quickly as possible, ideally no later than 24 hours, to avoid shaming the body by neglecting its required religious procedure. But, one must wait for the immediate family to arrive. The deceased is buried in a clean, white handmade shroud without pockets, the final symbol of life signifying that "one can't take anything with them."

The seven days following a person's death is a time of mourning known as "sitting *shiva*". This is a time when friends share meaningful stories with the relatives of the deceased and help them to cope by helping them to remember all of the positive memories that remain that death cannot erase.

The Festivals

The Jewish Sabbath, or *Shabbat,* is the seventh day of every week which is set aside for one to become recharged spiritually. Judaism does not have names for the days of the week, and therefore, Sunday is considered the first day to *Shabbat,* which causes the Sabbath to fall on Friday evening.

Judaism recognizes a number of religious festivals throughout the year. There are six biblical holidays, which are: Rosh Hashana (the New Year), Yom Kippur (Day of Atonement), Sukkot, (the holiday of Booths), Shmini Atzeret, Shavuot (Pentecost), Passover and two rabbinically mandated holidays: Purim (the holiday of Lots) and Hannukah

Rosh Hashana is the Jewish New Year. It occurs on the first day of the first month which is Tishrei. The name literally means "head of the year" and is mandated in Leviticus 23:24-25, with the sounding of the ram's horn (or *shofar)* as a day of remembrance and celebration. It is a time of introspection, to look back on the mistakes of the past year and to plan changes for the upcoming year. No work is permitted on this holiday and much of the day is spent in synagogue. On this day, Jews believe that God brings out his scales in order to weigh the deeds of every person. The way the scales tilt will determine a person's fate for the coming year.

Yom Kippur is not as much of a holiday, but a Sabbath with extra restrictions. All the things that one cannot do one Shabbat ar alos forbidden on this day with five extra restrictions: 1) no eating or drinking, 2) no sexual relations 3) no wearing leather shoes, 4) no anointing oneself with oil, 5) no bathing. This holiday occurs nine days after Rosh Hashana, on the 10th of Tishrei. The days in between the two are known as 'the ten days of repentance'. Yom Kippur was selected as the Day of Atonement because it remembers when God forgave the Jews for worshipping a golden calf. Moses had pleaded with God for forty days and forty nights to gain His forgiveness for his people for their idolatrous sin. On this day alone, the High Priest of the Temple in Jerusalem may enter the Holy of Holies to offer a spice sacrifice.

Passover is a widely celebrated holiday, which commemorates the liberation of the Jews from Pharaoh's bondage in the days of ancient Egypt. According to the Bible, Moses pleaded with Pharaoh to "let my people go." When Pharaoh refused, God sent a series of ten plagues upon the Egyptians. The last was the most terrible: every firstborn Egyptian was to die at the stroke of midnight on the 15th of the Jewish month of Nissan. Jews, on the other hand, were to mark their doors with the blood of a sacrificed lamb so that God could "pass over" the houses in which His people lived.

Since this holiday is considered to carry such import, rather than hosting the service in the synagogue, it is held at home, involving the people most involved in carrying on the tradition; the children. The special meal has a fixed order and is called a *seder.* A special prayer- book called a *haggadah* is used for the occasion. The Egyptians were so anxious to be rid of the Jews after being inundated by the 10 plagues they forced them to flee before their bread could rise. The flat, unleavened bread called *matzoh,* happily recreates the Jews' quick departure from slavery. Christians know this meal as The Last Supper. This is the meal that Jesus partook of before his execution by the Romans.

Shavuot commemorates the day the Jews received the Law of God and were taught that true freedom means being free to be themselves, to be happy and to be holy. After leaving Egypt, God told the Jews that it would take them 49 days to reach Mt. Sinai. On the 50th day, they were to be given the Torah.

Sukkot is the holiday that celebrates Jewish survival in the face of impossible odds. Under God's special care, the Jews spent 40 years wandering the desert before they could arrive at the Promised Land with the Torah after leaving Mt. Sinai. During this time, God fed the Jews with *manna* (bread from the sky) and for protection from the harsh sun, clouds followed the Jews on their journey. During the eight days of this holiday, Jews build small huts called *sukkahs*. The point is to exchange the security of a house for a frail structure, making one realize that one's ultimate protection comes from God.

Purim is a holiday that teaches Jews never to be silent in the face of those who want to destroy them. The story began when Esther became the wife of King Xerxes after he got rid of his wife because she did not obey him. Esther hid her Jewish heritage from the king, until she learned that one of his top advisors, Hamman, was planning a mass execution of Jews on a day of his choosing because Mordecai, a Jew, had refused to bow down to him. Esther revealed her heritage to the King who recognizes that Hamman deserves to be hanged. This holiday is celebrated with conspicuous consumption of wine.

Hannukah, or The Festival of Lights, celebrates the miraculous burning of one day's worth of oil to burn for eight days. Judah Maccabee led a revolt against Antiochus IV, who had ordered that the alter of the Jewish temple be desecrated by requiring the sacrifice of pigs (a non-kosher animal). Judah won back the temple and it was rededicated. The rededication required the lighting of the menorah, however there was only enough oil for one night. Miraculously, it burned for eight days.

SIKH PRAYER

You are the Lord, we pray to You.
You have favored us with our being and our body.

You are our mother and father;
we are Your progeny.
In Your Grace, lie many comforts and luxuries.

Nobody can ascertain the limits of Your Glory.
O' Lord, You are higher than the highest.
The whole creation rests upon Your support.

Whatever has sprung from You,
follows Your command.

God, Your ways are mysterious.
Pleads Nanak: "I'm your loving, ardent devotee".

SYMBOL OF SIKHISM

Reminding humanity that: "all must die",
The 'Khanda' represents the ultimate reality of
'death' that must consume all mortals:
an irrefutable TRUTH.

There are two swords on the sides, symbolizing temporal and spiritual powers, and the double-edged sword in the middle represents wisdom and knowledge; the 'circle' symbolizes death.

SIKHISM
at a glance

Sikhism is a monotheistic religion that was revealed to Guru Nanak, the Sikh Prophet, around 1501 C.E. It presents a unique message of love and tolerance for all humanity. Sikhism brought about a revolution by awakening the gullible, ignorant masses that were being exploited by the Hindu priestly class, the Brahmins, and who were oppressed by the tyranny of the Moslem invaders, the Mughals and the Afghans. Through the realization that all human beings are equal in the eyes of God, the subjugated masses rebelled against the status quo, stemming the tide of oppression for the first time in 3000 years of South Asian history. The Sikh Prophets, using the Divine Revelation of God's Word as their inspiration, changed the course of history of South Asia, and (by implication), of the history of the world.

In order to achieve success in their noble mission, the Sikh Gurus practiced what they preached. They sacrificed their own lives and embraced martyrdom. Their innumerable disciples emulated their example by becoming equally valiant, and by laying down their lives for righteousness. The entire history of Sikhism is replete with sagas of martyrdom, for nurturing the sapling, planted by the Gurus. The postulates of Sikhism emphasize that the ultimate goal of a human-being is not a vision of God that culminates in re-absorption of the individual into the absolute reality, but the emergence of a race of God-conscious people, who remain earth-aware and thus operate in the mundane world of phenomena, with the object of transforming and spiritualizing it into a higher and more abundant plane of existence. As the Sikh scripture declares, "The God-conscious person is animated with an intense desire to do good in this world."

Miracles

Miracles abounded in the life and times of the Founder, Guru Nanak through the Tenth Master, Guru Gobind Singh. Gurdwaras are now erected at places associated with these miracles, where the occurrences can be verified today.

- **The Indelible Imprint**: One of the most acclaimed of these is Panja Sahib, Pakistan, where Guru Nanak's hand left an indelible imprint on a rock in the village of Batala.

- **The Wall that Wouldn't Fall**: A weak wall, erected to kill Guru Nanak, while he sat near, stands even today, after five centuries.

- **Stone as Wax**: Guru Nanak's figurine has been framed in a rock, as if it were wax. Located in Ladakh region of Jammu & Kashmir, India.

- **Bitter into Sweet**: One branch of a tree gives sweet fruit, as a result of Guru Nanak's glance, while all other branches continue retaining their bitter nature. Location: Pilibhit, Uttar Pradesh in India.

- **The Mobile mosque**: A plate bearing reference to this incident, related with the visit of Guru Nanak, is preserved, reverentially, in Mecca, Saudi Arabia. Innumerable other miracles cannot be listed as well.

It is amazing to note that some two centuries before scientists had even discovered the telescope, Guru Nanak, through revelation and spiritual powers, determined that many other planets, suns and moons existed. Furthermore, he conclusively elaborated upon the complexities of the creation of the universe, as written in the Sikh Scripture. It is quite a coincidence that as we write this, newspapers in America corroborate his statement, made over five centuries, ago, regarding the possibility of the existence of many suns, moons and life on other planets.

The Guru & The Sikh

The founder of Sikhism, Guru Nanak Dev, was born in 1469 A.D., in Village Talwandi, near Lahore (now in Pakistan). Nanak was greatly inclined towards spirituality, even at a tender young age.

Guru, in Sikh terminology, means a Prophet and a world-teacher. In fact Sikhism is one of the world's prophetic religions in that its origins could be traced to a specific encounter with the Divine. Accordingly, one can draw a clear distinction between Sikhism and the eastern religions like Hinduism, Buddhism and Taoism, which have an anonymous mysticism as their source of validity.

Guru Nanak's encounter with God is described, metaphorically, in the *Janamsakhis* (textual-narrations, pertaining to his birth-lore) in the following words: "As God willed, Nanak, his devotee, was escorted to His presence, to the Divine Presence, and then a cup filled with Liquid of Immortality was given to him, accompanied by the command: Nanak, pay attention. This is the cup of holy adoration of my Name; drink it. I am with you, and you do I bless and exalt. Go, rejoice in my Name, the Name of God, and preach to others to do the same. Let this be your calling."

The term "Sikh" originates from ancient Pali texts, where the word "Sikho," is used to describe a 'searcher of truth'. A Sikh of Guru Nanak also strives to destroy the wall of nescience that separates him or her from Truth. "How will the Truth become known and how will the wall of nescience be pierced?" asks Guru Nanak in the first chapter of the Sikh scripture. He then answers: "It is possible, by following the Will of God and by being in tune with the Cosmic Law, we will be able to grasp Reality".

The Sikh Gurus wrote their revelations in various languages and dialects so they would be accessible to people without any intermediaries. Through this act, Sikhism rejected the priestly class of the time, which tried to control the religious practices of the people by writing all religious texts in Sanskrit, an ancient language that is difficult to understand. For the first time, a religion in the Eastern world offered access to God without the priestly class.

To understand the emergence and expansion of Sikhism, in true perspective, it is imperative that the prevailing conditions (and their ramifications) be studied.

Role of Women and Family

Islam and Hinduism were the two predominant faiths in the Indian subcontinent when Guru Nanak received his ministry from God. Hindus were engrossed in practices that are strongly condemned by Sikhism, such as idol-worship; female infanticide, sati (forcible burning of a widow on her husband's funeral-pyre) and the "devadasi" system, where girls who had attained puberty would be used to satiate the carnal desires of the Brahmin priests. Polygamy was rampant; a man could have as many wives as he desired, and innumerable concubines. Women widows could not remarry. Young teen-aged girls were married off forcibly. Women had no access to education. Animals and even humans, especially virgin teenage girls approaching puberty, would be considered "most acceptable to the presiding-deity" of a tribe or of a family.

Sikhs do not adhere to any of those practices because Guru Amar Das, the third Sikh Prophet, who was a great defender of women's rights, rejected them. He encouraged widows to remarry and banned the horrific practice of sati. Sikhs believe men and women are equal.

> "From woman, man is born; within woman, man is conceived; to woman he is engaged and married. Woman becomes his friend; through woman, future

generations come. When his woman dies; he seeks another woman; to woman he is bound. So why call her low? From her, kings are born. From woman, woman is born; without her, there would be no one at all." (SGGS pg. 473)

Woman, as per Mahan Kosh, have 32 virtues over men which include humility, selfless service, compassion, contentment, mercy, patience, and many others. It is perhaps because of these qualities that in many places in the Sri Guru Granth Sahib, when Gurus had to show their extreme closeness to God, they presented themselves as female.

> "The female is in the male, and the male is in the female. Understand this, O God-realized being! The meditation is in the music, and knowledge is in meditation. Become a devotee and speak the language of love, faith and trust (with, and in, God)" (SGGS pg. 879).

Basic Tenets & Theology

Sikhism is a monotheistic faith and a reveled religion which shares many similarities with the Semitic traditions such as Judaism, Christianity and Islam. However, Sikhism does not believe in the doctrine of Original Sin, nor the concepts of Heaven or Hell. Sikhism preaches that we are rewarded or punished, according to our actions in this lifetime; we reap what we sow. Human life is precious because it is our opportunity to meet God, while living on this earth. Through good actions and by endeavoring to love humanity, we achieve Self-Realization. God is not a distant reality but resides within us and pervades all of creation. God is both Immanent and Transcendent.

> "Some sing your praises thinking you are Transcendent; others praise you thinking you are Immanent". (SGGS).

Sikhs are distinct from Hindus and Muslims, from all angles, including religious practices, ceremonies, festivals, social customs and traditions.

> "Guru Nanak [the Sikh Prophet] recognizes no authority, no doctrine, except that directly revealed to him by God" (*SGGS* pg. 599).

Since the Gurus wanted to have an enduring impact, and not just a superficial one, it took ten Gurus a period of over 250 years to "condition the soul and spirit" of their followers, to face the tyrant rulers and the barbaric intruders with courage and fortitude. Cowardice and indifference was effectively replaced with courage and bravery. The basic tenets of Sikh Faith are prayer, meditation, honest living, generosity, compassion, sharing, humility and patience. Other important planks on which rests the Sikh Faith are equality of all religions, universal harmony, peace and tolerance. Service to humanity is emphasized.

Hair is a symbol of saintliness, and a reminder of God's design. It is incumbent for Sikh men and women to retain unshorn hair, and to refrain from adultery, the use of drugs and other intoxicants like alcohol, cocaine, tobacco, opium, marijuana, etc. Lust, too, has been termed an addiction. It is a major religious and spiritual diktat, for a Sikh not to live on alms or donations. Furthermore, a Sikh considers it to be a psychological trauma, and a social stigma, accepting monetary benefits, which one has not worked to earn.

Repudiation of Rituals

In Sikhism, there is no place for idolatry (statue, icons, symbols, or photographs) or human-worship. Ritualism and superficial fanfare related to ceremonies has been denounced. Superstitious beliefs related to so-called specific auspicious days and dates have been negated. The Gurus command that all days have been made by God; therefore, all are equally auspicious. All humanity is created by the Lord; therefore, all are equal. The time when one remembers God is auspicious and the place where one remembers God is sacred. No time or place can be sacred in of itself.

Non-Violence

Sikhs are a peace-loving people. Non-violence, which enforces a strict prohibition against the use of arms under any circumstances, however, has no place in Sikhism. The Sikh Prophet, Guru Gobind Singh, declares, "When all peaceful means fail, to take up the sword is a lawful imperative, to contain the oppressor". He further states, "I would confront and oppose that what is evil, to destroy it or to subdue it, or die fighting against it, with dignity."

The fifth and the ninth Gurus were Martyrs. The four teenaged sons of the 10th Guru were Martyrs (the younger ones, aged 7 and 9 were bricked alive while the older ones, aged 15 and 17, performed the supreme sacrifice on the battlefield, facing ruthless seasoned warriors), and they embraced death, as did innumerable of their followers, for upholding the birthright of their choice of practicing the religion of their choice. They preferred death to a life of slavery and subjugation. There is no sign of 'suffering' on the faces of the Martyrs; no repentance, no regrets.

The Scripture

The teachings of Sikh Gurus and Saints, in the form of poetic compositions have been compiled in the Sikh Scripture, the Sri Guru Granth Sahib (SGGS). This 1430 page volume is reverentially placed on an elevated pedestal in the Gurdwara (Sikh Church). The Holy Book was written, compiled and edited by the Gurus during their lifetimes. It is noteworthy that out of all the scriptures of religions of the world, it is the only scripture written by the same person who received the Revelation.

The Tenth and last Sikh Prophet, Guru Gobind Singh, transferred his authority to the Sikh scripture and to the collectivity of the committed Sikhs, known as the Khalsa. This is the condominium of Guru Granth and Guru Khalsa Panth. The spirit of the Ten Sikh Prophets resides in the mystic body of the Khalsa, while their light resides in the Sikh scripture. The Sarbat Khalsa, an assemblage of representative Sikhs from all over the world, takes major decisions affecting the Sikh nation in consonance with the teachings of the Sikh Gurus enshrined in Guru Granth Sahib. The Sarbat Khalsa has the responsibility to keep the Sikh personal law dynamic and address new issues as they arise.

The tenth Guru, in his wisdom, did not deem it appropriate to include his own autobiography or his poetic encomiums for God in the SGGS like his predecessors had. There is a lot of controversy about the contents of the Dasam Granth, and an overwhelming majority of Sikh Saints, theologians, scholars, and preachers maintain that several 'additions' were made to his original works by vested interests, with an ulterior motive of neutralizing the worldview that the Sikhs have a unique and distinct identity, thereby wrongly attempting to present the Sikhs as part of Hinduism.

'Gurdwara' (House of Worship)

Gurdwara, which literally means "a door to the Guru," is the focal point for all Sikh congregations. Guru Nanak, the first Sikh Prophet, established the institution to organize Sikhs on a local level. Since the Sikh doctrine does not allow separation between spiritual and temporal affairs, all political movements affecting Sikhs have been launched from Gurdwaras. Some of the best examples are the Sikh non-violent fight against British aggression in the 1920's and against Indira Gandhi's military rule, known as the Emergency, in the 1970's. Even though the latter affected the entire country, out of a country of almost one billion people, only the Sikhs, who are just two percent of the total population, found courage to oppose tyranny.

There is no ordained priestly class in Sikhism. All Sikhs are expected to read prayers, sing hymns and perform other services. Both women and men can participate in all services and can occupy any administrative positions. As a mark of respect, all devotees must enter the Gurdwara after taking off their footwear and with their heads covered. They bow in front of the Sikh scripture and then sit down to listen to the devotional hymns. We should remember that the act of genuflection in front of the Sikh scripture is not idol worship. A Sikh bows to the message contained in the scripture and not to a book. Genuflection in front of the Sikh scripture indicates submission to the Word of God. Later, the Congregation stands up in prayer and at the conclusion of the services, partakes of *langar*, which is any type of food prepared with love and devotion by the community.

The tradition of *langar* was started by Guru Nanak, and was institutionalized by Guru Amar Dass, the third Sikh Prophet. All were required to partake of *langar.* Before this policy was put into effect, many Hindu Brahmins would come and meet the Guru, but not eat with the "lower-caste" women and men in the Guru's congregation. This bold initiative ended the Brahmins' hypocrisy and confirmed equality between all humanity, as all were forced to eat together. Even the Mughal Emperor Akbar partook of *langar* while sitting on the floor with the common people before he could meet with the Guru. Langar inspires and promotes the spirit of disinterested action, *sewa*, in a Sikh and therefore must be cooked by the community and cannot be catered from a restaurant. By catering the food, an artificial distinction between rich and poor is created. Such a distinction repudiates the very purpose of *langar* and is antithetical to Sikhism. The Gurdwara services are performed on all occasions: birth, naming, graduation, commencement of a business-venture, baptism, during weddings, thanksgiving and during sad occasions such as death. The entire Congregation, without distinction of class or creed, enjoys equal status and all are required to sit on the floor to partake of the holy food. No Gurdwara, anywhere in the world (and there are several thousands of them) has been recorded as having been "closed" or "sold." This is a very unique aspect of the followers of Sikhism, who are famous for sacrificing their all for the welfare of humanity.

Contributions of the 10 Sikh Gurus

As it has been asserted before, the Sikh Scripture declares that the Ten Sikh Gurus were a manifestation of one Divine Light that passed on from one prophet to the next. Even though they changed bodies, the light remained intact and they preached the same message throughout the 250 years of their sojournings on this earth.

Guru Nanak Dev, Sikhism's founder, brought about a revolution in the Eastern world. He opposed tyranny and exploitation. He rebelled against futile practices, empty rituals and superstitions. God sent him as a Prophet to reveal Sikhism to humanity. Guru Nanak was probably the first Human Rights activist known to the Eastern world. The ruling emperor, Babur, imprisoned him when he opposed tyranny of the invader. of Sikhism, as declared by Guru Nanak pronounced three fundamentals; they are: (1) business should be done with integrity, (2) God should be kept in mind throughout all one's endeavors, (3) charity should be extended to the poor. Guru Nanak was exceedingly pluralistic and welcomed all facets of mankind towards and Sikhism and as God's children.

Guru Angad Dev, the second Sikh Prophet, gave definitive shape to a new alphabet, Gurmukhi, that was to replace all existing scripts. The new script was easy to read and the common people, without the use of any intermediaries, could now read and understand Guru Nanak's message. He also strengthened the Sikh congregations and preached God's revelation relentlessly.

Guru Amar Das, the third Sikh Prophet, was a great defender of women's rights. Over thirty percent of the preachers appointed to preach the message of Sikhism were women. He also appointed female bishops. He institutionalized the Sikh tradition of Langar or community kitchen, and enforced equality in all Sikh congregations. He encouraged widows to remarry and banned the horrific practice of sati, where women are forced to be burned with the funeral pyre of their dead husbands.

Guru Ram Das, the fourth Sikh Prophet, founded the spiritual Sikh capital, Amritsar, and started work on the world-famous Golden-Temple, to place emphasis upon the spiritual way of living. His hymns, as recorded in the Sikh scripture, have the breathtaking theme of humility.

Guru Arjan Dev, the fifth Sikh Prophet, was a literary-giant, who undertook the work of compiling the Sikh scripture. He included the hymns of Hindu and Muslim saints without discrimination in the Sikh scripture. He was martyred for refusing to embrace Islam. The extent of barbaric-torture was such that he was boiled in a cauldron containing water, and hot sand was poured upon his head, during scorching summers. Nonetheless, he prayed blissfully.

Guru Hargobind, the sixth Sikh Prophet, was groomed by Guru Arjan to become a warrior-saint. He implemented Guru Nanak's doctrine of double-sovereignty that deems spiritual and temporal affairs of equal importance. A Sikh must strive to excel both spiritually and temporally, always subordinating politics to ethics. The Guru created the Sikh seat of sovereignty, the Akaal Takhat, which is comparable to the Vatican. However, the head of the Akaal Takhat is just a mouthpiece of the Sikh commonwealth, and all of his directives must be a result of decisions taken by the Khalsa Panth, the committed Sikhs all over the world.

Guru Har Rai, the seventh Sikh Prophet, had Guru Hargobind order him to maintain an army to fight oppression and to continue his mission of preaching the word of God. Arms were to be used as a last resort when all peaceful means of reaching a resolution had failed. He pioneered Ayurvedic which is free health care.

Guru Harkrishan, the eighth Sikh Prophet, was appointed Guru when he was barely five years old. He led the masses with grit and determination, displaying rare spiritual-acumen, wisdom and sagacity. He departed from the mortal world at the age of eight, proving that age has no correlation with spiritual power, as prophecy is God's gift, bestowed upon whomsoever God deems worthy. This also is an excellent example of equality, bestowed by the Sikh doctrine, on all human beings.

Guru Tegh Bahadur, the ninth Sikh Prophet is one of the greatest defenders of freedom ever known to humankind. He preached against the Hindu caste system and repudiated the superiority of the Hindu priestly class. When the Brahmins were being proselytized to Islam and came to him for help, he gave them a helping hand, and embraced martyrdom. Long before Voltaire was to say, "I might not believe in what you say but I will fight till death for your right to say it," the Guru showed the world that freedom of practice was a cherished gift that ought to be defended. The Guru was a great warrior, but he gave his life peacefully.

Guru Gobind Singh, the tenth and the last Sikh Prophet, gave up everything in his fight against oppression. He sacrificed his four sons, his parents and gave his own life while preaching the message of love. "Hear ye all, I proclaim the truth, only those who love will find God". The Guru was a prolific writer, a poet, a great warrior, a musician, a chef, and had innumerable other talents. His greatest accomplishment was his non-attachment to this world and his ordination committed Sikh, the Khalsa.

The Vaisaakhi of 1699 : Beginning of a Revolutionary Era

The manner in which Guru Gobind Singh gave proof of his thorough knowledge of the art of dramaturgy on the Baisakhi day is fairly well known. He asked for a 'head,' when a brave individual offered his head. This man was taken into the Guru's tent, and when the Guru returned with a blood-soaked sword, he asked for another head. The audience was stunned, but when he asked for another and then another, individuals volunteered. He repeated the call a total four times more. Finally, he brought out the five men, and still alive, to the amazement of those onlookers. The five were then administered what is known as the Baptism of the Double-edged Sword (khande di pahul), and were then knighted as Singhs, the Five Beloved Ones; they were the original constituents of the Order of the Khalsa, into which the Guru himself begged to be admitted, and was initiated as the sixth. On that day, a milestone in Sikh history, Guru Gobind Singh transformed Sikhism by giving it its modern form. The most prominent element that this Guru initiated was the five articles of faith. They prescribe that Sikhs wear: (1) unshorn hair, (2) a small wooden comb for the hair, (3) a steel bracelet; its symbolism is in the fact that it is round pointing to the fact that reality is without a start and without a finish, (4) a ceremonial sword pointing to Sikh's dedication to strive for fairness and truth, and (5) knee-length under-shorts attempting to uphold the value of a disciplined life-style so dear to a Sikh's heart. Guru Gobind Singh proclaimed a formal code of conduct that forbids adultery and promiscuous sexual behavior, use of drugs and intoxicants, cutting of hair from any part of one's body, female infanticide and consumption of sacrificial meat. Hair, being sacred, was to be kept covered at all times. This required the wearing of turbans and scarves, which are also signs of sovereignty.

Ceremonies & Festivals

The religion of Sikhism notes four momentous episodes in one's life: birth, initiation, marriage, and death. The importance of birth and death in an individual's existence are clear. "Amrit', the Initiation ceremony, marks the commencement of 'the journey' symbolizing the aspirant's first step as per the Sikh 'way of life'. Those who have taken Amrit are called the Khalsa. 'Anand Karaj', or marriage, is another significant ceremony. It is a public commitment by two Sikhs to walk on the path of Guru Nanak throughout their lives. The marriage ceremony becomes a spiritual journey undertaken by two lovers of righteousness, striving to achieve Self-Realization.

All other ceremonies, whether child naming, graduation, starting a business-venture or employment are, inevitably, marked by a gathering of relatives and friends at a Gurdwara. Holy hymns are recited and Langar is served to the guests.

The major festivals of the Sikhs are "Hola Mohalla," which is celebrated in March, to observe the change of season by indulging in sports and revelry and "Baisakhi". "Diwali", in November, is celebrated to mark the occasion when the sixth Guru secured the release of 52 kings from the prison of India's Mughal Emperor, Jehangir.

A Brief Sketch of Sikh History

In 1710, a republic was established under Baba Banda Singh Bahadur in the Moghul Empire found in present day India. At that time, the farming areas were handed over to farmers and then he announced throughout the land that everyone is part and parcel of the state; everyone is equal. Subsequently, he proclaimed that power was not something held over a people, but something that emanates from the people, and hence, was the possession of the people.

For fifty years, through heartless and appalling maltreatment with the sole intent of a mass genocide, not only did the Sikhs turn down the cruelty of the oppressive Muslim regime, but refused to abandon their cry: "We want liberty or death!" As the battles came to a close, their freedom and liberty was reinstated. Sikh's took control of the government and the Sikh Commonwealth was established from the middle of the 18th century for about 100 years. This eventually developed into the Sikh Empire, called SarkariKhalsa,

For this extended period of time, the Sikh Empire continued all the way from the middle of India to Afghanistan and spreading east as far as Tibet. Unfortunately, the British army assailed the Sikh Empire towards the middle of the 19th century in the Anglo-Sikh wars. To the Sikhs credit, as one historian notes, they "brought the British and their Hindu mercenaries to their knees every time." In pre-British India, the powerful Sikh Emperor, Maharajah Ranjit Singh, is renowned for having sanctioned grants of cash, gold, and land for Hindu Temples, Christian Churches, and Muslim Mosques. He had, under his employ, European courtiers and generals, besides people from all religions and races in India

Before India gained its independence in 1947, many Sikhs took part in the fight for independence. Their active cooperation was enlisted by the Congress Party, which was spearheading the movement under the stewardship of Mahatma Gandhi. At this juncture, promises pertaining to Sikh identity, representation and autonomy, were made by the Congress Party. The Sikhs believed these promises, and plunged head-on into the arena. From the over two thousand killed in the fight for Indian independence, over fifteen hundred of them were Sikhs: an astonishing number when we take into consideration what percentage of Indian are Sikhs! Similarly, from the more than 2500 prisoners sentenced to life, over 2000 of them were Sikhs. Also, from the more than one hundred-twenty Indians executed through hanging at the hands of the British, again over eighty percent of them were Sikhs. In fact, historians and British archives have noted that Sikhs heroically chose death over apologizing and having their lives spared for their insurrections in India.

Ever-since independence in 1947, there has been well-thought out indirect attacks at the Sikh sub-culture attempting to cause the Sikh religion, its values and political influence to dissolve. Even other minorities (Christians and Muslims) in India have been subjected to maltreatment at the hands of the majority. Even though the writers of the Constitution pledged to write it with the consent and approval of the Sikh minority, this promise was not kept three years later. There was not any mention of Sikh autonomy within the framework of the Constitution. As a consequence, even though Sikhs played an integral role in freeing India, the promise of Sikhs' rights to sovereignty and autonomy was quickly forgotten. A constitution was framed paving the way for a decidedly centralized government run by the majority of Indians, completely denying any Sikh religious identity or political sovereignty.

Continued frustration due to unfulfilled promises made by the Indian government starting in 1947, led the Sikhs to start a peaceful movement, resulting in several thousand Sikh locked up in Indian jails over the span of a quarter of a century. To crush the non-violent independence movement, the government deployed ruthless tactics. In retaliation to the injustice meted out, this agitation assumed the form of a Sikh independence movement with the desire of breaking away from the Union of India. In 1984, an army operation was launched on the Golden Temple and 37 other Sikh shrines, killing several thousand Sikhs. Over 200,000 innocent Sikhs were killed in the aftermath of this operation, and thousands are still languishing in jails, without trial. The paradox of this injustice is that even two decades later, thousands of Sikh widows still pine for justice, whilst the murderers were given Ministerial berths. The Indian State has subdued all attempts by Amnesty International and local human rights groups like the People's Commission.

Section 1

ONE CREATOR

Is there a God? In the Jewish tradition this is not a valid question, nor is the Western philosophical tradition needed to prove His existence. Actually, in all books of the Bible, God's existence and providence are taken for granted. While the Jewish story tellers fill in the gaps of how Abraham, the first Hebrew, came to recognize God's existence, the Bible itself refrains from such philosophical speculation. It is unnecessary and would be foreign to the Bible's purpose. It is not clear how Abraham came to recognize God: what is a compelling thought, an ephemeral feeling, or was he just born with the belief? This is never clarified. The Bible and Judaism take as their starting point the belief in God. All investigations come after this one basic assumption. This assumption is the basis for Judaism and monotheism.

Judaism repeatedly emphasizes that God is good. If God were a human being, perfect goodness is not a trait that we could expect of Him. In the course of history, mankind has unfortunately been able to testify to the truth of Lord Acton maxim: "Power corrupts; absolute power corrupts absolutely." Having experienced some really tyrannical and authoritative monarchs and governments, it is remarkable that Abraham gave us not only the gift of belief in one God, but the concept of ethical monotheism as well. In fact, the very word 'God', in English, is a contraction of the longer word "good". God, who could be anything, chose to be good. So strongly does Judaism hold this to be true that the Bible records one of the most remarkable debates between the Almighty and man.

Theologians ask: If God wants people to believe Him, why doesn't He manifest Himself clearly and unambiguously? Why doesn't He appear in full resplendent glory, so that no one could ever dispute His existence? The answers, however, are undesirable.

God is an experience of affirmation of hope and peace, of a blissful radiance and fragrance. God is serene tranquility.

God is the paramount power, the insurmountable. He is beyond the experiences of life and death, of joy and sorrow, of victory and defeat. And, God is beyond the realms of human knowledge and comprehension. He is attainable by virtue of His own grace (if that is forthcoming from Him) being bestowed on a devotee. He cannot be reached by persistence and penance. Meditation is the sunlit-path to the glorious destination. God is Omnipotent, Omnipresent and Omniscient. He is all pervasive, in creations and creatures, in all mass and matter, in space and in water, on land and in the air. He is, in essence, in each particle and in each atom. Therefore, the inference is that God is Transcendental & Immanent, both, at once, simultaneously. Before the Creation was effected, God was present, all by Himself, in a self-absorbed state of being.

"He has no form, no shape, no color; God is beyond the three qualities. They alone understand Him, O Nanak, with whom He is pleased." [SGGS 283].

"God is beyond the limitations of form or shape, or of social class or race. These humans believe that He is distant; but He is quite obviously and apparently very close (in fact He resides within each creature). He enjoys His presence in every heart, and no filth sticks to Him, and He is blemish-less. He is the blissful and infinite primal Lord; His light is all pervading. Among all divine beings, He is the most divine, Creator-architect, rejuvenator of all. How can Nanak's single tongue worship and adore Him? He is the eternal, imperishable Entity. One whom He unites with the True Guru — such a person's generations are redeemed. All His servants serve Him, and Nanak is the most humble servant at His door." [SGGS 1096]

GOD IS ONE

"Listen Israel: The Lord is our God; the Lord is one." (Deut. 6:4)

Judaism began with Abraham, who recognized one God as the Creator of the world.

"Have we not all one Father? Did not one God create us all? Why then does each man betray the other profaning the covenant of our forefathers?" (Malachi 2:10)

The 'Big Bang' theory of creation, accepted by most scientists today, agrees with the Judaic teaching that the universe came into being "out of nothingness, out of a void" (*ex nihilo*), but does not venture to offer any judgment about how it happened.

It insists that God, the Creator is, undoubtedly, "only one." This monotheistic belief outright rejects the "many gods" of paganism, the "three persons" of the Trinity, and the "two gods" of dualism.

God is also the Caretaker. He is a God who maintains a close, ongoing personal relationship with every one of His creations. Ethical monotheism views the all-powerful God as a being who, voluntarily, chooses to be guided solely by the principles of truth, kindness and justice.

GOD IS ONE

"God is One, His Name is Truth, He is the Creator, He is the fearless One, He does not bear animosity towards anyone, He is beyond the cycle of birth and death, and He is the benevolent grace." [SGGS 1]

"As much as the word of God is in the mind, so much is His melody; as much as the form of the universe is, so much is His body. He is the tongue, and He is the nose. Do not speak of any other. My Lord and Master is One (God). He is the One and Only; He is the One alone, proclaims Nanak." [SGGS 350]

"The various gods and goddesses, in various religions and cultures are, in reality, only mere manifestations of the One and Only God. He Himself is the Doer of deeds." [SGGS 908]

"The One and Only Creator of the universe is all-pervading. All shall once again merge into the One. His One form has one, and many colors; He leads all according to His One word." [SGGS 1310]

"Describe the Lord as the One, the One and Only. How rare are those who know the taste of this essence. The Glories of the Lord of the Universe cannot be known, proclaims Nanak: He is totally amazing and wonderful!" [SGGS 299]

The emphasis is on the message of One God. Hence, the various manifestations of the powers of God cannot be misconstrued as being God. They only represent certain attributes of God, which emanate from Him, and could never be an independent 'persona' or entity.

GOD IS TRUTH

"But the Lord, God, is truth; He is the living God, and the Everlasting king. The land will tremble from His anger, and the nations cannot take his wrath." (Jeremiah 10:10)

"Many days passed for Israel without a true God, without a teaching priest, and without Torah." (II Chronicles 15:3)

"Pilgrimages, austere discipline, compassion and charity—these, by themselves, bring only an iota of merit. Listening and believing with love and humility in one's mind, one cleanses oneself with the Name, at the sacred shrine deep within. All virtues are the Lord's, humans have none at all. None has the ability to decipher the Lord's coded limits. The time of the Creation of the Universe is not known to any religious Priests, or to the Yogis. One who claims to know everything shall not be decorated in the world hereafter." [SGGS 4]

To realize and to know truth, the exact nature of falsehood needs to be understood in the correct perspective.

"False are body, wealth and all relations. False are ego, possessiveness and Maya (Illusion). False are power, youth, wealth and property. False are sexual desire and wild anger. False are chariots, elephants, horses and expensive clothes. False are deception, emotional attachment and egotistical pride. False is self-conceit. Only devotional worship is permanent, constant and Truth. Nanak lives by meditating on the Lotus Feet of the Lord. False are the ears, which listen to the slander of others. False are the hands, which steal the wealth of others. False are the eyes, which gaze, stealthily upon the beauty of another's wife. False is the tongue, which enjoys delicacies and external tastes. False are the feet, which run to do evil to others. False is the mind, which covets the wealth of others. False is the body, which does not do good to others. Without understanding, everything is false. Blessed is that body, says Nanak, that remembers the Lord's Name." [SGGS 268]

The Supreme One is a reality. Truth, fact or reality exists at two planes: mental and material. Mind observes the universe through the medium of the senses, and all that is observed is a reality. Matter, too, is a realistic-entity. And, human beings are a combination of mind, matter, spirit and intelligence. All of these, together, constitute Truth. God, alone, is the undisputed, unchallenged, Truth.

GOD IS THE CREATOR

"In the beginning, God created the sky and the land." (Genesis 1:1)

"These are the products of the sky and the earth when they were created on the day that the Lord, God, made the land and the sky" (Genesis 2:4).

"Don't you know? If you haven't heard: the Everlasting God, the Lord, the Creator of the land's ends, will not get tired, nor weary. There is no way to evaluate the depth of His understanding." (Isaiah 40:28)

"I, the Lord, am your Holy One, the Creator of Israel, your King." (Isaiah 43:16)

"Remember your Creator in the days of your youth, before the evil days come, and the years arrive when you shall say, I have no desire." (Ecclesiastes 12:1)

"His word created everything." [SGGS 3]

God is the creator of nature. God's grace is also part of His nature; so:

"By His nature we see, by His nature we hear; by His nature we have fear, and the essence of happiness. By His nature the nether worlds exist, and the ethereal ones; by His nature the entire creation exists. By His nature the Holy Scriptures of the Hindu, Jewish, Christian and Islamic religions are compiled. By His nature all deliberations are held. By His nature we eat, drink and dress; by His nature all love exists. By His nature come the species of all kinds and colors; by His nature the living beings of the world exist. By His nature virtues exist, and by His nature vices exist. By His nature come honor and dishonor. By His nature wind, water and fire exist; by His nature earth and dust exist. Everything is in Your nature, Lord; He is the all-powerful Creator. His Name is the holiest of the holy. Says Nanak: Through the command of His will, He beholds and pervades the creation; He is absolutely unrivalled." [SGGS 464]

"He fashioned the creation; seated within the creation, He beholds it with delight. He is the giver and the creator; by His pleasure, He bestows His mercy. He is the knower of all; He gives life, and takes it away, again with a single word (command). Seated within the creation, He beholds it with delight." [SGGS 463]

"He himself is the Creator. Everything that happens is His doing. There is none except Him. He designed the creations; He beholds it and He understands it. Says servant Nanak: The Lord is revealed to the aspirant-soul, who is God-loving, such a one is the living expression of the Guru's word." [SGGS 12]

GOD IS GRACIOUS

"He (Jonah) prayed to the Lord saying: Please Lord, isn't this what I wanted when I was still in my land? Because of this I hastened to escape to Tarshish, for I knew that You are a God of graciousness, mercy, slow to anger, great kindness, and relent on evil." (Jonah 4:2)

"When you (Israel and Judah) return to the Lord, your brothers and your children will find mercy by their captors, so that they will return to this land; for the Lord your God is gracious and merciful; He will not turn His face from you if you return to Him." (II Chronicles 30:9)

When God informed Abraham that He is about to destroy the cities of Sodom and Gomorrah, for their wickedness, Abraham had the audacity to question the Lord's action: "Will the judge of the whole world not act justly?" Abraham wondered how God could annihilate the innocent along with the wicked, without differentiating between the two.

Steeped as we are in millennia old traditional thinking that God is righteous, we are inclined to disbelieve that God could be unjust and act unfairly. Imagine how imprudent it must have been for Abraham to challenge God's sense of justice. Had Abraham put forth the identical question to a mortal king, the king would feel no necessity to justify his actions, let alone alter them. Even though Abraham accepted God as the Creator of the whole universe, he was unwilling to believe that this same God might act in an unjust fashion! God, for a Jew, can be held for his commitment to justice. What is even more striking is the fact the God agreed with Abraham's viewpoint.

"True is the Master, true is His Name—speak it with infinite love. People beg and pray, and the Great Giver distributes His gifts so very magnanimously and in abundance. So, what offering can we place before Him, by which we might have an exclusive audience, with Him? What words can we speak to evoke His love? In the ambrosial hours before dawn, chant the True Name, and contemplate upon His glorious greatness. By the karma of past actions, the magnificently exquisite robe (this physical body) is obtained. By His grace, the Gate of Liberation is found. Know this well: the True One Himself is all." [SGGS 2]

"His blessings are so abundant that there can be no written account of them. The Great Giver does not hold back anything. There are so many great, heroic warriors begging at the door of the infinite Lord. So many creations contemplate and dwell upon Him, that they cannot be counted. So many perish, engaged in corruption. So many enjoy His bounties, and then deny receiving. So many foolish consumers keep on consuming. So many endure distress, deprivation and constant abuse. Even these are Your gifts, O Great Giver! Liberation from bondage comes only by Your will. No one else has any say. If some fool should presume that he does have a say, he shall learn, and feel the effects of his folly. He Himself knows, He Himself gives. Few, and rarest of the rare, are those who acknowledge this." [SGGS 5]

God clarifies the matter before Abraham. Given a certain minimum number of righteous people among the residents of these wicked cities, then God would not destroy them.

"The Rock: His actions are perfect for all His ways are justice. A God of faith, lacking all iniquity; He is righteous and upright." (Deut. 32:4)

When Moses asks God to share with him His essence, God passes before Moses and reveals His attributes: "The Lord, the Lord, is a God of mercy and graciousness, slow to anger, with much kindness and truth. He extends kindness to the thousands, forgives inequity, negligence, and sin…" (Exodus 34:6-7)

"Everyone makes mistakes, but God and His messengers are infallible." [SGGS 60]

"Do not blame the sovereign Lord; when someone grows old, his intellect leaves him. The blind man talks and babbles, and then falls into the ditch. All that the perfect Lord does is perfect; there is not too little, or too much. Says Nanak: The God-loving person merges into the perfect Lord." [SGGS 1412]

Do not become like the infirm or the blind, while you have all faculties, intact, to reason out issues.

This unison and harmonious blend between God and man, is termed; communion. In such a state, one does not criticize God's decisions and refrains from denying His existence.

"The supreme Lord, the transcendent Lord, the True Guru, saves all. Hence, it is unbecoming to criticize God's decisions, his ways and his works. Says Nanak: Without the Guru, no one crosses over the turbulent life-ocean; this is the perfect essence of all contemplation." [SGGS.611]

Section 2

****

REDEEM YOURSELF

****

"The Lord, God, formed man, from dust of the ground, and He blew into him the soul of life; man became a living animal: (Genesis 2:7)

"Make me (Isaac) savory food that I love; bring it to me so that I may eat. For that, my soul will bless you (Esau) before I die." (Genesis 27:4)

"When you take a census of the people of Israel, according to their numbers, every person must give a ransom for his soul to the Lord, when counting them. Then, there will not be a plague among them when counting them." (Exodus 30:12)

"When a soul sins: if he heard the voice of swearing, and he is a witness – whether he saw or knew of it – if he does not utter it, then he shall bear his iniquity." (Leviticus 5:1)

"If the priest buys a soul with his money, he (the layman) may eat of it (holy food). Also, those born in his house may eat of his food." (Leviticus 22:11)

"The Lord, your God, will circumcise your (Israelites) heart and the hearts of your children so that you love the Lord, your God, with all your heart and with all your soul, so that you may live." (Deuteronomy 30:6)

"When my (Jonah) soul fainted, the Lord I remembered; my prayer came to You, to Your holy Temple." (Jonah 2:8)

"Let the enemy chase after my soul and overtake it, and crush my life into the land, and rest my honor in the dust forever." (Psalms 7:6)

"My portion is the Lord, says my soul, therefore I hope in Him." (Lamentations 3:24)

"By His command, bodies are created; His command cannot be described. By His command, souls come into being; by His Command, glory and greatness are obtained. By His command, some are high and some are low; by His written command, pain and pleasure are obtained. Some, by His command, are blessed and forgiven; others, by His command, wander aimlessly forever. Everyone is subject to His command." [SGGS 1]

"Says Nanak: That Lord alone is the Husband of all. She, upon whom He casts His glance of grace, becomes the happy soul-bride." [SGGS 351]

"The chamber of the soul is so dark, without the Name of the Lord." [SGGS 355]

"Without the Name, the soul does not even exist." [SGGS 354]

"My soul does not stay held by the Merciful Lord. It is greedy, deceitful, sinful and hypocritical, and totally attached to worldly attachments." [SGGS 360]

"But the soul is neither young nor old, O siblings of destiny." [SGGS 378]

"Forever and ever, the soul is illumined; in the Saadh Sangat congregation, the company of the holy." [SGGS 378]

"Crimson, crimson, crimson — this is the color of the soul-bride who is imbued with the love of her beloved." [SGGS 739]

"The account is kept for every second, every instant; the soul suffers for the bad and the good. O Nanak, the angelic beings are united with the word of the God; this is the way God made it." [SGGS 1110]

“The bramble said to the trees: ‘If in truth you anoint me to be king over you, then come and take refuge in my shade. But if not, then fire will come forth from the bramble and devour the cedars of Lebanon.’” (Judges 9:15)

“Do not trust their lying words when they say: ‘the Temple of the Lord, the Temple of the Lord, the Temple of the Lord are these.’” (Jeremiah 7:4)

“Woe to the serene in Zion and to the secure in Mount Samaria. They are deemed chief of the nations, but the house of Israel came to them.” (Amos 6:1)

“Do not believe in a friend; do not trust in an official; guard the openings of your mouth from those who lie in your bosom.” (Micah 7:5)

“And I will leave in your midst a poor and destitute people, and they will have refuge in the name of the Lord.” (Zephaniah 3:12)

“Worship in purity lest He becomes angry, and you lose the path, as His anger will blaze but in a moment. Praiseworthy are all those who take refuge in Him.” (Psalms 2:12)

“Two hundred twelve were all that were chosen as gatekeepers of doorways of the gates were. These were registered by their genealogy in their villages; they were whom David and Samuel the seer established in their office of trust.” (I Chronicles 9:22)

TRUST

"The Name of the Lord, is a jewel, a ruby. It brings Truth, contentment and spiritual wisdom. The Lord entrusts the treasures of peace, intuition and kindness to His devotees. This is the treasure of my Lord. Consuming and expending it, it is never used up." [SGGS 893]

"I worship the One who is worthy of being worshipped. I trust the One who is worthy of being trusted. Like water merging in water, I merge in the Lord. Says Jai Dayv: I meditate and contemplate the Luminous, Triumphant Lord. I am lovingly absorbed in the Nirvaanaa of God." [SGGS 1106]

"Kings, rulers and monarchs enjoy pleasures and gather the poison of the wealth of others. They do not trust their own children or spouses; they are totally attached to the love of Maya." [SGGS 1245]

"Why keep what is held in trust for another? Giving it back, peace is found." [SGGS 1249]

"But there, in the court of the Lord, all beings will be judged. Those who have violated the people's trust will be disgraced; their noses will be cut off." [SGGS 1288]

"When I call, answer me, God of my righteousness; when in distress, You have eased me; be gracious to me and hear my prayer." (Psalms 4:2)

"The Lord heard my supplication; the Lord will accept my prayer." (Psalms 6:10)

"A prayer of David: Hear O Lord righteousness, listen to my entreaty, give ear to my prayer from lips without deceit." (Psalms 17:1)

"Listen to my prayer Lord, and give ear to my cry; to my tears do not fall silent, for I am a stranger with You, a resident like all my forefathers." (Psalms 39:13)

"The sacrifice of the wicked is an abomination to the Lord; but the prayer of the upright is His want." (Proverbs 15:8)

"One who removes his ear from hearing Torah, even his prayer is an abomination." (Proverbs 28:9)

"Even though I scream and cry out, He shuts out my prayer." (Lamentations 3:8)

"You covered Yourself in a cloud that prayer cannot pass." (Lamentations 3:44)

"I (Daniel) set my face to the Lord God with fasting, sackcloth, and ashes, in order to utter prayer and supplications." (Daniel 9:3)

"The Lord appeared to Solomon by night, and said to him, 'I have heard your prayer, and I have chosen this place as my house of sacrifice.'" (Chronicles II 7:12)

"Praying for anything other than Your Grace, O Lord, leads me from one problem to another. Bless me that the hunger in my mind is quenched, once and for all." [SGGS 958]

The three pillars of the Rock-like steadfast "Monument of Prayer" are: service, meditation, and total surrender of one's ego.

God confers solace and fearlessness. Prayer is an essential ingredient of the "Faith-in-God" Doctrine, which emphasizes that God is, always, right. Doubt should not be permitted to creep in, on this count. Hence, one must pray to God, the source and the light, at all times, day or night, in joy or sorrow, and on all significant occasions, like birth, naming-ceremony, wedding, death, commencement of educational or business ventures. Pray to God, at all times, in prosperity or adversity. The concept of prayer is engrained in the Sikh psyche and belief-structure. It says that God is not a law of nature, alone, nor of Karma, or of pre-determination, alone. It is, in essence, all of these, together, and even much more. His grace can modify/amend the negative-writ, to rescue the bereaved one, who is, now, praying and wailing, in agony, for help. The Savior is omnipresent and all pervasive. Hence, we see that God is transcendental and immanent, both, at once. After crossing the barriers, hindrances and obstacles of physical desires, material gains and mental traumas, one is forced to (there's no alternative available, there's no other strategy to be employed) pray to the Lord, for express grant of sublime and pristine grace. This, then, is the finality of spiritual elevation. Prayer, when coupled with sincere meditative-contemplation, becomes an extremely potent force that could radically alter the prevailing scenario, thereby bringing about a positive transformation, in the life of the devotee. The deity is in the heart and soul, and is not to be searched, anywhere else.

"When Pharaoh will say to you (Moses): 'Give a sign'; then, you will say to Aaron, 'Take your staff and toss it before Pharaoh.' It shall become an alligator." (Exodus 7:9)

"When Moses extended his hand over the sea, the Lord moved the sea with a strong Eastern wind all night, and he made the sea into land and the water split."(Exodus 14:21)

"As all the people that have seen my (God) glory and my miracles, which I did in Egypt and in the desert, and have, nevertheless, tested me these ten times, and have not listened to my voice…" (Num 14:22)

"And His signs and His actions that He did in Egypt for Pharaoh, king of Egypt, and to all his land." (Deut 11:3)

"… the great trials that your eyes saw, the signs and great wonders." (Deut 29:2)

"The waters that were descending from upstream stood still and rose up in one column..." (Joshua 3:16)

"On that night, the Lord's angel went out and slaughtered one hundred eighty-five thousand of the Assyrian camp. When the rest awoke in the morning, everyone was corpses." (II Kings 19:35)

"Without enshrining God's name in the heart, miracles and occultism is futile and undesirable." [SGGS 593]

"If one were to become a Siddha (a celibate, a monk) and work miracles, summon wealth and become invisible and visible at will so that people would hold me in awe and esteem, one might go astray and forget the Lord, and His exalted Name would not reside in his mind." [SGGS 14]

Without godly grace and meditation upon His Name, the mind's wild horses shall never rest in tranquility and peace. All miracles are God's handiwork. Success in performing miracles on a superficial plane, does not have any linkage with being a spiritually inclined and/or a religiously oriented individual.

The spiritual power of performing miracles has been used by the great masters, over the ages, all over the world, for the spread of the gospel and the word of God, and the universal message of love and compassion, peace and harmony.

Healing of the tormented mind and the haunted soul, too, has been an important field, where the real Godheads and pious ones have worked wonders, without expecting recognition or reward, power or position for themselves. This classification of miracles is the one required by humanity, in this age of hatred, infested and ridden with violence and greed. The Sikh-Gurus, Hindu Saints and Muslim Pirs whose verses have been included in the Sri Guru Granth Sahib, as well as other mystical-spiritual leaders were vociferously against the negative forms of miracles, not subscribing to the idea that someone possessing miraculous powers would, necessarily, be an enlightened soul. Of course, there could be enlightened souls having powers, but they do not exercise these powers, for they feel that would be tantamount to interference in Godly regimentation, laws, discipline, natural order.

"In the end of the day, when everything has been considered: fear God and safeguard his commandments, for this is all man has to do." (Ecclesiastes 12:13)

"'Do I need all these sacrifices?' said the Lord. 'Am I sated with burnt offerings of rams, and the fat of fed beasts? I do not want the blood of bulls, lambs, or goats.'" (Isaiah 1:11)

"May the Lord fulfill His purpose for me. O Lord, Your kindness is eternal; do not forsake the works of your own hands." (Psalms 138:8)

"Can you understand the depth of God? Can you find the purpose of God?" (Job 11:7)

"I said in my heart: 'God will judge both the righteous and the wicked, for there is a time for every purpose and for every work there.'" (Ecclesiastes 3:17)

"O man you were sent here to gain merit, but you are engrossed in futile activities, and your time is running out." [SGGS 43]

"First, the baby loves mother's milk; second, he learns of his mother and father; third, his brothers, sisters and aunts; fourth, the love of play awakens. Fifth, he runs after food and drink; sixth, in his sexual desire, he does not respect social customs. Seventh, he gathers wealth and dwells in his house; eighth, he becomes angry, and his body is consumed. Ninth, he turns gray, and his breathing becomes labored; tenth, he is cremated, and turns to ashes. His companions send him off, crying out and lamenting. The swan of the soul takes flight, and asks which way to go. He came and he went, and now, even his name has died. O Nanak, the self-willed egoistic persons love the darkness. Without the Guru, the world is drowning."[SGGS 137]

The ideals or purposes, of life, undergo a rapid transformation, in consonance with the change and variance in socio-economic and politico-religious environment and conditions, cultural background, levels of education/literacy, God-gifted talents and intelligence, and of course, with advancing age. Hence, it can be safely inferred and assumed that the purpose of life, for an infant, would surely differ from that of an adult or of an aged-person. Priorities shift automatically, in accordance with the change in scenario. Another significant determining factor is that the human species has come of age after millions of years of evolvement, commencing the journey from the most primitive of creations of the Lord almighty. Advances achieved by humans are really commendable, but, in the process, God and spirituality have been relegated to the back seat, with an increasing interest in materialistic values, and pleasures of the senses, which are momentary (sexual-promiscuity, addictions, an insatiable lust and appetite for wealth and power, even at the cost of the annihilating life, on earth.)

"Salvation belongs to the Lord; your blessing is upon your nation forever." (Psalms 3:9)

"Who knew that Israel's salvation would come out of Zion? When the Lord shall bring back the captives of his people, Jacob shall rejoice, and Israel will be happy." (Psalms 14:7)

"Also he will be my salvation; for a hypocrite cannot come before Him." (Job 13:16)

"It is good to silently hope for the salvation of the Lord." (Lamentations 3:26)

"Sing to the Lord, all the land; tell of his salvation from day to day." (I Chronicles 16:23)

"I will trust in God, my savior, and I will not be afraid; for the Lord is my strength and my song; He is my salvation." (Isaiah 12:2)

"Truly from falseness he worshipped in the hills, and from the many mountains; truly in the Lord, our God, is the salvation of Israel." (Jeremiah 3:23)

"As for me, with a voice of thanks I will sacrifice to you. That which I have promised, I will repay, as salvation belongs to the Lord." (Jonah 2:10)

"One who, in his soul, loves the will of God, is said to be liberated while yet alive. As is joy, so is sorrow to him. He experiences eternal bliss, and is not separated from God. As is gold, so is dust to him. As is ambrosial nectar, so is bitter poison to him. As is honor, so is dishonor. Such a one treats a pauper and a king alike. Whatever God ordains, is acceptable to such a person." [SGGS 275]

"The soul-bride is in love with her Husband Lord; she focuses her consciousness on the word of the Guru's holy hymns. The soul-bride is joyously embellished with the gift of intuition; her hunger and thirst are taken away." [SGGS 993]

Great emphasis has been laid upon the Doctrine of "Attunement-with-God" (entering into the realm of God-consciousness). This belief relates to the transmigration of the soul, and salvation, thence, would mean total release from the vicious cycle of birth and death. Salvation could be attained, even in the present lifetime, here and now, on our very own planet, instead of the imaginary heavens, after death. It is very much possible that such an ecstatic level or plane is arrived at, but the only condition is that utmost restraint is required to be exercised, over the reins of the wild horses of the senses. "Parampad" (the 4th and highest state of the mind) is, in effect, the quintessential "salvation". The lower three states are: the waking-state, the dream-state, and the dreamless-sleeping-state. Salvation means loving God, with all the intensity and faith, at one's disposal, so as to arrive in the fragrantly wonderful zone of "Communion with God". Grace and benediction and benevolence play a far significant role, than Karma alone, towards the realization of this objective. Emancipation is very much possible right here, provided the pleader is sincere in his prayer, approach and inclination and motives.

"And a pure man should gather the heifer's ashes, and remove them to outside the camp, in a pure place, and it will be a safekeeping for the congregation of the people of Israel for a water of sprinkling; it is for purifying." (Numbers 19:9)

"And you must immerse your clothes on the seventh day, and then you will be purified, and then afterward you may rejoin the encampment." (Numbers 31:24)

"The priests and the Levites purified themselves and they purified the nation and the gates and the wall." (Nehemiah 12:30)

"When the hands and the feet and the body are dirty, water can wash away the dirt. When the clothes are soiled and stained, soap can wash them clean. But when the intellect is stained and polluted by sin, it can only be cleansed by the love of the Name. Virtue and vice do not come by mere words; actions repeated, over and over again, are engraved on the soul. One is bound to harvest what one sows. Says Nanak: By God's Command, we come and go in reincarnation." [SGGS 4]

"When the mind is filthy, everything is filthy; by washing the body, the mind is not cleansed. This world is deluded by doubt; hardly anyone understands this. O' mind, chant the one Name. The True Guru has given this treasure. Even if one learns the Yogic postures of the Siddhas, and holds his sexual energy in check, still, the filth of the mind is not removed, and the filth of egotism is not eliminated. This mind is not controlled by any other discipline, except the Sanctuary of the True Guru. Meeting the True Guru, one is transformed beyond description. Prays Nanak: One who dies upon meeting the True Guru, shall be rejuvenated through the word of the Guru's Shabad. The filth of attachment and possessiveness shall depart, and the mind shall become pure." [SGGS 558]

Just as nobody prefers to sit in close proximity to a person wearing unwashed clothes, similarly a person with a 'sullied' thought-process is shunned by all and sundry for he spreads vitriolic words around, thereby vitiating the environment.

God blesses us in every sphere of life, and by meditating upon His Name, our sagging spirits are rejuvenated, and we are saved. In the company of the holy, filth is washed away. The supreme Lord becomes our companion and benefactor. Continuing to meditate, the primal-being is sure to become the protector, everywhere and for all times to come.

"The wicked does deceitful deeds; but he who sows righteousness receives the true reward." (Proverbs 11:18)

"Jonathan said to the youth carrying his armor: 'Come let us go over to the garrison of these uncircumcised; maybe the Lord will perform a deed for us, for the Lord has no restraints in saving either many or few.'" (I Samuel 14:6)

"For God will consider every deed in judgment – even deeds done in secret - whether good or evil." (Ecclesiastes 12:14)

"Jacob's sons returned from the field when they heard it [what had happened to their sister]; and the men were grieved, and they were very angry, because he had done a vile deed in Israel in lying with Jacob's daughter; which thing ought not to be done." (Genesis 34:7)

"Whoever saw [the twelve pieces] said, no such deed was done nor seen from the day that the children of Israel came up from the land of Egypt until this day…" (Judges 19:30)

"Behold, I will rouse them from the place that you sold them, and will return your deed upon your head." (Joel 4:7)

"Look at the nations, take note and be utterly confused, for I will perform a deed in your days that you will not believe when it is recounted." (Habakkuk 1:5)

"Brother, understand the Lord's sense of justice: as one sows, so does one reap." [SGGS 308]

"Nobody is to be blamed, except one's own actions. Whatever misdeed one performed, for that one has suffered; so, do not blame anyone else." [SGGS 433]

"All creatures are under the supreme command. According to His will, He commands them. His pen writes out the account of everyone." [SGGS 1241]

God driveth according to His will; the present life circumstances/conditions that one finds oneself embroiled in, may be attributable to, and traceable to, the innumerable acts of commission and omission during the past life/lives. These may be construed to be in the form and shape of rewards, or penalties, as the case may be. Virtuous deeds, in this lifetime, have the potential of presenting a human being with the invaluably cherished gift, of being spared the agony and ignominy of undergoing transmigration.

"The deluded ones have forsaken God the primal being, the life of the world, and they have come to rely upon mere mortals. In the love of duality, the soul-bride is ruined; around her neck she wears the noose of death. As one sows, so shall one harvest; your destiny is recorded on your forehead." [SGGS 134]

Worthy deeds (performed on the physical-plane) that are visible to the human-eye, are appreciated and recognized by God, in the form of worldly prestige and honor, that is, also apparent and obvious, to everyone. Honorable deeds on the spiritual plane (that cannot be viewed, even under the most advanced microscope), shall be credited to the account of the pious soul, who shall become the deserving recipient of magnificent accolades and encomiums, in the world, hereafter.

There is an exemplary account about Abraham's ideal servitude towards God, through his service and compassion for fellow humans. It happened when God was visiting Abraham during the latter's recuperation from his circumcision.

While playing host to God, Abraham noticed three strangers, apparently Arabs weary from long and dreary travels, desperately looking for food and shelter. Abraham left God and went out to provide hospitality to these three. At first glance, it would appear to be a horrendous perversion of priorities: men over God! But, Abraham understood that God, being so great, is never in need of people; mortals in need of help should be taken care of if God is to be served. In fact, Abraham did the greatest service of God by tending to the Arab's needs.

The Talmud says: 'Whosoever saves one life, it is as if he saved the entire world." This is based on the premise that the world started with "one life". Every human killed is a potential Adam, by himself. Kill a person and you destroy an "entire world'.

"Woe to the builder of his house without righteousness, and his attics without justice; who works his friend without wages, and does not recompense him for his deeds." (Jeremiah 22:13)

"They set the priests in their groups and the Levites in their divisions in the service of God in Jerusalem, according to that which is written in the Book of Moses." (Ezra 6:18)

The Lord inspires the aspirant to serve Him (by believing in His Existence). None else can do it. Such a one is His devotee, who is pleasing to Him. God blesses him with His love. God is the great giver, ever so very wise. There is no other like Him. He is the all-powerful Lord and Master; nobody knows how to worship Him. His Mansion is imperceptible. For ordinary mortals, it is so difficult to accept His will. Says Nanak: I have collapsed at Your door, Lord. I am foolish and ignorant — please save me." [SGGS 1185]

"The wandering beggars, warriors, celibates and hermit, through the perfect Guru, consider this: without selfless service, no one ever receives the rewards." [SGGS 992]

"That selfless servant, who lives in the Guru's household, is to obey the Guru's commands. He is not to call attention to himself in any way. He is to meditate constantly within his heart on the Name of the Lord. One who sells his mind to the True Guru — that humble servant's affairs are resolved. One who performs selfless service, without thought of reward, shall attain his Lord and Master. He Himself grants His grace; Says Nanak: That selfless servant practices the Guru's teachings and preaching." [SGGS 286]

"This body is softened with the Guru's word: One shall find peace, in selfless-service. The entire world continues to be affected by the force of reincarnation. Perform selfless-service, and you shall be given a place of honor in the court of the Lord. Declares Nanak: Now, swing your arms in joy!" [SGGS 25]

Sharing is a basic tenet of Sikh faith. Cooking and serving holy food to the congregation, washing utensils and dusting the shoes of the devotees, is one kind of service; and there is also the service of patients, disabled and aged.

"Sons of man: until when will you allow My glory to turn to shame, and love futility and seek falsehood forever?" (Psalms 4:3)

"By one who withholds love due to his friend, or forsakes the fear of God." (Job 6:14)

"My beloved is mine and I am His, the shepherd of roses." (Song of Songs 2:16)

"You are completely beautiful my love; there is no blemish in you." (Song of Songs 4:7)

"How beautiful and lovely you are, love of delights." (Song of Songs 7:7)

"For all this I paid attention to and sought to understand it all: that the righteous, the wise, and their deeds are in God's hand; also love and hatred man does no know, everything is before them." (Ecclesiastes 9:1)

"I (Nehemiah) said: 'Please Lord, God of the Heaven, the great and awesome God, keeper of the covenant, of bestowing grace to those who love Him and safeguard His commandments.'" (Nehemiah 1:5)

"Jehu son of Hanani the Seer went out to greet him, and said to King Jehoshaphat, 'Are you going to help the evil, and love the haters of the Lord? Because of this, there will be a plague upon you from the Lord.'" (II Chronicles 19:2)

"A man's friend is befriended, and there are lovers closer than a brother." (Proverbs 18:24)

The power of love has the potential of significantly changing one's overall perspective, for the betterment of self, and others. This new outlook could achieve wonders in all spheres of human endeavor. All religious and spiritual deeds, sans Love, shall be rendered purposeless, in fact they shall be said to be exercises-in-futility. Love develops gradually, over a period of time, in everybody's life, as per varying circumstances, experiences and conducive-environment. Various instances of love can be cited, in the natural-realms. The blossoming of flowers, and the buzzing around of the bumblebee, are two examples. The peacock-dance is famous, at the sighting of rain clouds. The love-pangs emanating from the heart of the timid partridge, pining for the full moon, are all manifestations of the hidden love, that is sublime and pristine, elevated and selfless, true and sacred. Love is such a magnetic force, which attracts and influences everyone. Love is a state of mind. Its born inside the human heart, grows and develops, and on attaining maturity, assumes the form of affection, and the whole personality undergoes a metamorphic sea-change. The body and the mind, the heart and the soul, all, start reverberating with spiritually gifted strains of mellifluous music. An unparalleled and inexplicable feeling of exhilaration engulfs the person. Anyone, who has never had this experience, this boon, is really an unfortunate and condemned mortal. Loving humanity, is loving God.

“Nobody is to be considered an enemy, and one should not harbor animosity towards anyone. God, who expanded His expanse, is within all; this is the teaching imparted by the True Guru. Be a friend to all; when the sense of separation is removed from the mind, then unity with the Lord becomes easy, for the stubbornness is gone, ambrosial nectar rains down, and the word of the Guru’s holy hymns seems sweet. He is pervading everywhere, in the water, on the land and in the sky; Nanak beholds the all-pervading Lord.” [SGGS 671]

"From Zion, the perfection of beauty, God appears." (Psalms 50:2)

"I perceived a boundary to all perfection, but your commandment is wide." (Psalms 119)

"He sets an end to darkness, and investigates every all perfection: the stone of darkness and the shadow of death." (Job 28:3)

"All travelers clap their hands at you; they hiss and shake their head at the daughter of Jerusalem: 'Could this be the city that men call the perfection of beauty, the joy of the whole earth?'" (Lamentations 2:15)

"A lover of discipline is a lover of knowledge; but a hater of reproof is a boor."(Proverbs 12:1)

"He uncovered their ears to discipline, and said return from iniquity." (Job 36:10)

"Do not delay in practicing righteousness; delay in committing sins. Implant the Name of the Lord, within oneself, and abandon greed. In the Sanctuary of the Saints, the sinful residues of past mistakes are erased. Meditating on the Lord, one shall become steady and stable. Nanak meditates on the Lord, for nothing and none else is permanent/stable, everything being variable, fluctuating, oscillating and temporary." [SGGS 1354]

There is none who could lay claim to achieving perfection, for God is the only perfect One. Beholding his ambrosial glance, one becomes saintly. Endless are his virtuous qualities, and his worth cannot be appraised. One who pleases him is united with Him. The tongue is one, but His praises are countless. The True Lord of perfection cannot be assessed, is incomprehensible, balanced in the state of Nirvaana. He is not sustained by food; He has no hatred or vengeance; He is the giver of peace. Countless devotees continually bow in reverence to Him. In their hearts, they meditate on His lotus feet. One must always strive to enshrine His pure thoughts in one's mind, to attain a blessed life. Only God, does not contract or expand, He does not become small or big, and, hence, is complete, total and the only perfect One. Anything incomplete becomes an eyesore, whether it's a statue, machinery, or furniture, because in that state it is of no consequence, and of no avail, for it cannot be put to any usage. An incomplete work of music, dance, prose or poetry is futile, as it cannot be enjoyed by anybody.

The entire universe is functioning in consonance with the laws and discipline, enshrined in the unwritten constitution of the nature, authored by God. Bricks must be laid out, in a certain mode or array, in order that a straight wall be raised. And, all mechanisms must function in accordance with a planned structure or design, involving operations and optimum utilization and desired results.

FORGIVENESS, COMPASSION & SHARING

"With You there is forgiveness so that you may be feared." (Psalms 130:4)

"Mercy and forgiveness are attributed to the Lord our God, for we have rebelled against Him." (Daniel 9:9)

"Remember Your compassion and Your kindness Lord, for they are eternal." (Psalms 25:6)

"God's kindness has not ceased, nor is His compassion exhausted." (Lamentations 3:22)

"The Lord, God of their forefathers, sent to them through His messengers, from early morning, for He had compassion on His people and on His dwelling place." (II Chronicles 36:15)

"Saul said: 'Blessed be you unto the Lord, for You have shown me compassion.'" (I Samuel 23:21)

"May You forgive Your people who sin against You, and all their transgressions against You. May You make their captors feel compassion towards them when they are taken captive." (I Kings 8:50)

"It will come happen that after I remove them, I will have compassion and return each man to his heritage and each man to his land." (Jeremiah 12:15)

"No eye pitied you to do any of these to you, to show compassion to you; but you were cast into the open field, for you were loathed, on the day you were born." (Ezekiel 16:5)

Sikhism FORGIVENESS, *COMPASSION & SHARING*

"My Lord forgives innumerable sins, in seconds." [SGGS 260]

"To practice forgiveness is the true form of fasting, good conduct and contentment. Disease does not afflict one, nor does the pain of death. One is liberated, and absorbed into God, who has no form or feature." [SGGS 223]

"Without patience and forgiveness, countless hundreds of thousands have perished. Their numbers cannot be counted; none could count them. By the blessing of the Lord's word, enter the mansion of the Lord's presence; one shall be blessed with patience, forgiveness, truth and peace. And one shall be unfettered. Partake of the true wealth of meditation, and the Lord Himself shall abide within one's body. Through egotism, one is distracted and ruined; other than the Lord, all things are corrupt. Forming His creatures, He placed Himself within them; the Creator is unattached and infinite." [SGGS 937]

"Make compassion the cotton, contentment the thread, modesty the knot and truth the twist. If this is the sacred thread that the priest has to offer, for the soul, then one must wear it. It does not break, it cannot be soiled by filth, and it cannot be burnt, or lost. Blessed are those mortal beings, says Nanak, who wear such a thread around their necks. One buys the ordinary thread for a few shells, and seated in an enclosure, one wears it. Whispering instructions into others' ears, the priest becomes a guru. But the recipient dies, and the sacred thread falls away, and the soul departs without it." [SGGS 471]

"One who works for what he eats, and gives some of what he has, says Nanak, he knows the path." [SGGS 1245]

Compassion and contentment are intertwined-entities. Both lend discipline to life.

"When they are humbled, you would say: 'Get up! Those with troubled eyes, He will save.'" (Job 22:29)

"Moses and Aaron came to Pharaoh and said to him, 'This is what the Lord, God of the Hebrews, said: 'Until when will you refuse to humble yourself before Me? Send out My people go so that they may serve Me.'" (Exodus 10:3)

"Fear of the Lord is a discipline in wisdom, and humility precedes honor." (Proverbs 15:33)

"The man Moses was more humble than any other man on the face of the earth." (Numbers 12:3)

"Before man's end, his heart grows haughty, and humility precedes honor." (Proverbs 18:12)

"The result of humility is fear of the Lord, wealth, honor and life." (Proverbs 22:4)

"All the humble of the land that has acted according to the law should seek the Lord: seek righteousness and seek humility…" (Zephaniah 2:3)

"You (Israelites) should remember the way that the Lord, your God, led you these forty years in the desert, [that He did this] in order to humble you, and to test you, in order to know what is in your heart, whether you would keep his commandments or not." (Deuteronomy 8:2)

"One must become as humble as grass, if one longs to enter the Court of the Lord, as grass is cut, trampled over and remains under others' feet." [SGGS 1378]

"The simmal tree is straight as an arrow; it is very tall, and very thick. But those birds, which visit it hopefully, depart disappointed. Its fruits are tasteless, its flowers are nauseating, and its leaves are useless. Sweetness and humility, says Nanak, are the essence of virtue and goodness. When something is placed on the balancing scale and weighed, the side that descends is heavier. The sinner, like the deer hunter, bows down twice as much. But what can be achieved by bowing the head, when the heart is impure?" [SGGS 470]

"Among all persons, the supreme person is the one who gives up his egotistical pride in the company of the holy. One who sees himself as lowly, shall be accounted as the highest of all. One whose mind is the dust of all, recognizes the Name of the Lord in each and every heart. One who eradicates cruelty from within his own mind, looks upon the entire world as his friend. One who looks upon pleasure and pain as one and the same, affirms Nanak, is not affected by sin or virtue." [SGGS 266]

If one becomes the slave of the Lord's slaves, then he finds the Lord and eradicates ego from within. The Lord of bliss is his object of devotion; night and day, he sings the glorious praises of the Lord. Humility must not be misconstrued to imply timidity and weakness. It is, on the contrary, a powerful characteristic, that speaks volumes about the humble one's personality. The humble person is bestowed fame and fortune, even without asking (praying) for it. On the other hand, someone who seeks recognition, on account of one's wealth, status or knowledge, is not a humble person. Occasionally, one needs to remind oneself of the destructibility of the human-body (by looking downwards, towards the earth, and at the dust and ashes, unto which this body shall merge).

"He (God) will say: 'I will hide My face from them (Israelites) and see what will be their end, for they are a backward generation, children who have no faith.'" (Deuteronomy 32:20)

"The people that gave the money did not ask the workmen for an accounting, for they acted in good faith." (II Kings 12:16)

"However, no accounting should be made with them of the money given to them, for they act in good faith." (II Kings 22:7)

"His (the king's) soul is defiant and is not on a straightforward path. But, the righteous will live by his faith." (Habakkuk 2:4)

"One who has faith in the Guru comes to dwell upon God. He is acclaimed as a devotee, a humble devotee throughout the three worlds. The Lord resides in his heart. True are his actions; true are his ways. True is his heart; Truth is what he utters. True is his vision; true is his form. He distributes Truth and he spreads Truth. One who recognizes the supreme Lord as the True One, that humble being immerses himself, in meditation, and merges his identity with the sole entity." [SGGS 283]

And, this trust prods one onto realization of the self, and one's roots, which ultimately results in God-realization.

"One must try, always, to remain in a state of equilibrium and stability, and never to let dilemma invade the mind. That's possible only when one tends to have an abiding faith in the Guru's sayings (word/ command/advice). On that foundation is the marvelous palace, having bejeweled walls, raised. Such a devotee is entitled to be the recipient of lavish eulogies and encomiums, all over, on the surface of earth, and has a rare and unique glow and radiance, on his face." [SGGS 678]

Just as faith in water leads one to the realization that one's thirst will be quenched upon drinking it. Similarly, just as faith in the sun reassures the needy that its warmth will provide mental comfort when faced with a cold, chilly night in the dead of winter. Faith in the supreme-reality leads one to the fulfillment of all worldly desires. And, finally, this faith and trust assist the bearer, to be ferried across the Ocean-of-Fire (life), in a befitting and honorable fashion. This would be salvation, for an aspiring soul.

"Why have we fasted and you did not see? Why have we afflicted our soul and you did not know? On your fast days, you pursue your business and extort exact all your debts." (Isaiah 58:3)

"The men (spies) answered her (Rahab): 'We will die in your place if you do not tell over our business. It will be, when the Lord gives us the land, we will act kindly and truly to you.'" (Joshua 2:14)

"If you restrain your foot because of the Sabbath, and from pursuing your own business on My holy day; if you the Sabbath 'a delight,' and the holy day of the Lord 'honored'; you will honor it by refraining from doing your own ways, nor by pursuing your own business, nor speaking of mundane matters." (Isaiah 58:13)

"Make all deals, O traders, and take good care of the merchandise. Buy that object which will go along, to the next world. In the next world, the All-knowing Merchant will take this object and shall reward the earthly trader. Take the merchandise of the Lord's praises along. The Lord shall see this and approve. Those who do not have the assets of Truth—how can they find peace? Like the deer caught in the trap, they suffer in terrible agony; they continually cry out in pain. The counterfeit coins are not put into the treasury; they do not obtain the blessed vision of the Lord-Guru. Practicing falsehood again and again, people come and go in reincarnation, and forfeit their honor. Advises Nanak: Those who chant the Name of the Lord earn great profits." [SGGS 22]

"Praise the formless Lord in the mind. O my mind, make this the true occupation. Let the tongue become pure, to taste the ambrosial nectar. And then the soul shall be, forever, peaceful. The company of the holy is the all-important one. Hence, perform the tasks assigned by the Lord, and listen to the Lord's sermon. In the Lord's court, such a face shall be radiant, so promises Nanak." [SGGS 81]

"With greed within them, their minds are filthy, and they spread filth around. They indulge in filthy deeds, and suffer in pain. They deal in falsehood, and nothing but falsehood; telling lies, they suffer in pain. Rare is that person who enshrines the immaculate Guru's word within his mind. By Guru's grace, his skepticism is removed. He walks in harmony with the Guru's will, day and night; remembering the Name of the Lord, he attains peace." [SGGS 1062]

An ideal business is in which society benefits from its profits. Such a businessperson is God's chosen one. His service to humanity and his humanism shall be the cause of receiving rewards, forever, financially, and spiritually.

Section 3

****

THE OPPOSING FORCES

****

"The salvation on that day was turned into mourning for all the people, for the people heard on that day: 'the king (David) is saddened over [the death of] his son." (II Samuel 19:3)

"He (Elazar son of Dodo) got up and fought the Philistines until his hand became weary and his hand cleaved to the sword. The Lord brought about a great victory that day. The people came after [with nothing to do] but plunder [the dead]." (II Samuel 23:10)

"He (Shammah son of Agei) stood in the middle of the field and defended it. He repelled the Philistines. The Lord brought about a great victory." (II Samuel 23:12)

"Sing a hymn to the Lord, a new song, for He has done wonders. His right hand and His holy arm have brought about victory for Him." (Psalms 98:1)

"Only though [implementing wise] strategies can you make war, and victory comes when there is many counselors." (Proverbs 24:6)

"To You, Lord, is greatness, might, splendor, victory and majesty, for all that is in heaven and earth is Yours. To You, Lord, is the kingdom and You are exalted over all as a head." (I Chronicles 29:11)

"Please [Bilham son of Peor], come now and curse this nation (Israel) for they are mightier than me (Balak son of Zippor). Maybe I can attack them and drive them from the land, for I know that which you bless, is blessed, and that which you curse, is cursed." (Numbers 22:6)

"When, by His grace, the True Guru is met, the lamp is lit within the temple of the mind and it realizes what victory/defeat really are, then he comes to appreciate the true value of his own home." [SGGS 235]

"Time and time again, dwell upon the Lord. Dwelling upon the Lord, defeat shall not come to you. I am a sacrifice, a sacrifice to those, who sing the praises of the Saints, the sons of the Lord. Meeting the Lord, total Truth is obtained." [SGGS 342]

"He has no pain — he is totally at peace. With his eyes, he sees only the One Lord. No one seems evil to him — all are good. There is no defeat — he is totally victorious." [SGGS 1302]

'The noose of death is cut; one's wanderings cease; victory is obtained, when one conquers his own mind; eternal stability is obtained from the Guru, and one's day-to-day wanderings cease." [SGGS 258]

"That which is for his good, he thinks evil. If someone tells him the truth, he looks upon that as poison. He cannot tell victory from defeat. This is the way of the faithless cynic." [SGGS 180]

"Celebrate the victory of the Lord; taking to His sanctuary, the supreme status is obtained. I am a sacrifice to the feet of the True Guru. The Guru is the boat; through the Shabad of His word, the terrifying world-ocean is crossed over." [SGGS 414]

"Holding them by the hand, He has lifted them up out of the deep, dark pit, and their victory is celebrated throughout the world. He elevates and exalts the lowly, and fills the empty. They receive the supreme, sublime essence of the ambrosia of the Name." [SGGS 804]

God is both a Mother and a Father figure. It is fascinating to note that one of the Hebrew names of God is '*Shekhina*,' which symbolizes the physical manifestation of God's presence on earth. It has long been noted by Kabbalists and exegetes that this name of God is a feminine noun. On the other hand, one of the most common names for God in the Bible, '*Elohim'* (and most other names of God as well) are masculine words. This dichotomy is not surprising. One would expect God to exemplify characteristics generally associated with both males and females. For example, the most holy name of God, the Tetragrammaton (YHVH), refers to God's characteristic of mercy. A merciful God is more in consonance with feminine or motherly instincts. On the other hand, the name of God that we mentioned above, *Elohim*, is associated with God's characteristic of justice. A strict God, always following the letter of the law and not falling to merciful whims, is more in tune with attributes of a father-figure. The Jewish concept of a Lord/God is a combination of female and male attributes. The Almighty is both a 'He' and a 'She', thereby harmonizing the best of both genders, so that humans can feel blessed with both, a Mother and a Father in heaven and on earth. One's mortal parents act as God's 'authorized representatives' on earth, to bear and rear children. The Heavenly parents, on the other hand, assume charge of the offspring for all time.

There's a Jewish proverb that states: "Without woman, man is only half a man; he is incomplete." Eve was meant to be man's closest mate, taking away the existential loneliness experienced by Adam on his first day of existence. More than this, she would fulfill her Biblically designated destiny of being '*Ezer Ke-negdo'*, a helpmate for man (Genesis 2:20).

Rabbinic commentators note that the latter word '*Ke-negdo'* could be translated as against him, implying that woman must sometimes act against her husband. This is because woman is meant to balance out the deficiencies in man's nature with her feminine attributes. She was to be different than man. Man and woman are to be complementary.

FEMALE & MALE

Woman and man are complements, as well as supplements to each other. The mutual attraction between the two magnetic fields is natural, because man has certain female hormones/genes in him, and vice-versa.

"The female is in the male, and the male is in the female. Understand this, O God-realized being! The focus of attention is on the celestial music of God's Noumenon, resulting in the realization of Almighty's power." [SGGS 879]

The insatiable appetite for power and authority has led man to assume the leadership-roles in a variety of spheres of endeavor, namely politics, religion, business, warfare, and the larger society, in general. Some thinkers and philosophers, naturally men, had the courage to classify women as "Insignificant, irrelevant ones". Women were castigated, oppressed, subjugated, tortured, exploited in all manners, possible, and were relegated to the background, in all matters.

Guru Nanak was the first religious preacher who raised his voice against the tyranny and indignation suffered by women, over the ages.

"Woman bears a male child; within woman, man is conceived; to woman he is engaged and married. Woman becomes his friend; through woman, the future generations come. So why call her low? She gives birth to kings. From woman, woman is born; without woman, there would be no one at all. Only the True Lord is excluded from the womb's cycle of birth and death." [SGGS 473]

The woman's contribution to society cannot and must not be ignored. Her role has to be recognized by the male populace. The human frame is a temple, constructed by God Himself, and the home is a temple of understanding, created jointly, by woman and man. Only when mutual love and care are shared with humility and grace, witnessing God in each other, shall their home and family be blessed, where peace, harmony, serenity and tranquility shall prevail.

"When a man marries a woman and lives with her, if she does not find favor in his eyes - for he finds an immoral matter about her – he should write for her a bill of divorce, give it into her hand, and send her out of his house." (Deuteronomy 24:1)

"Fire consumed His young men, His young ladies lacked marriage songs." (Psalms 78:63)

"Solomon made a marriage alliance with Pharaoh, king of Egypt. He took Pharaoh's daughter and brought her to the city of David, until he finished building his house, the Lord's house and the surrounding wall of Jerusalem." (I Kings 3:1)

"Jehoshaphat possessed abundant wealth and honor; he allied himself by marriage with Ahab." (II Chronicles 18:1)

"If he takes a second wife; her food, her garment, and relations may not be diminished." (Exodus 21:10)

"If a man seduces a woman that he is not engaged to, and lies with her, he must provide her with a marriage contract [if she wants to marry this man and her father approves]." (Exodus 22:15)

"I (God) saw that even though I divorced faithless Israel for committing adultery, and had given her a bill of divorce, nonetheless, her sister Judah was not afraid; she also went and played the harlot." (Jeremiah 3:8)

As per Sikh customs/traditions as governed by the religious-spiritual Diktat of the Gurus, woman and man undertake to tie the nuptial-knot according to the prescribed code-of-conduct. They must reciprocate love and understanding, while taking due care to recognize each other's uniqueness, thereby ensuring equality (as equals, and as life-partners). This shall eliminate any occurrence of conflict on the basis of a perceived threat to either's identity. Harmony shall prevail, and all crisis situations shall be dealt with, in a spirit of compromise and commitment, keeping divorce at bay. The ascending divorce-rate in the Western society and culture, is attributable to the fact that the institution of marriage is considered to be no more than a legal contract, that can be nullified, with the stroke of the pens of the two parties and a Judge. Both must strive to achieve a state of camaraderie on all planes: emotional, physical, financial, intellectual, and spiritual. Celibacy has been repudiated in the strongest terms, for it is well nigh impossible to banish the thought of sexual-union.

To have religious sanction, the ceremony is to be solemnized in the presence of the holy congregation, where the bride and the groom are required to circumbulate the Scripture four times, as the priest reads the appropriate hymn.

"In the first round, the Lord sets forth instructions for performing duties of married life. Embrace the conduct of righteousness, renouncing sin. Enshrine the contemplative remembrance of God, in your hearts. Second round, the Lord leads both to meet the True Guru, the primal being. The fear of the fearless Lord in the mind eradicates the filth of egotism. The bride prepares to start a new life, in a new home, on leaving her parental abode. Third round, the mind is filled with Divine love. In the fourth and final round, the emphasis is on unison, between the spouses, as also communion between God and human-soul. She has attained her Lord and Master, the cherished fruit of her mind's desires." [SGGS 773]

"I (God) call upon heaven and earth to testify this day about you (Israelites) that I have set before you life and death, blessing and cursing. You should choose life so that both you and your offspring may live." (Deuteronomy 30:19)

"The Lord, God, formed man from the dust of the ground, and breathed into his nostrils the soul of life. Man then became a living animal."(Genesis 2:7)

"In the six hundredth year of Noah's life, in the second month on the seventeenth day of the month, all the springs of great depth burst forth. The windows of heaven were opened [and all mankind and animals died]." (Genesis 7:11)

"One who strikes another so that he dies is put to death." (Exodus 21:12)

"When I realized that you were no savior, I put my life into my own hands, and crossed over against the Ammonites, and the Lord delivered them into my hand…" (Judges 12:3)

"You will make known to me the path of life, the way fullness of joy in Your presence is, the pleasures of Your right hand forever." (Psalms 16:11)

"He (Isaac) said: 'I am old and I do not know the day of my death.'" (Genesis 27:2)

"Now, please forgive my (Pharaoh) sin this one time, and pray to the Lord, your God, that He may remove from me this death only." (Exodus 10:17)

"Only this is the chance, a golden one at that. Just ponder, and analyze, hypothetically, this very moment, for later you might lose this opportunity, and then, nothing more than a sordid feeling of remorse and repentance shall remain, in the heart." [SGGS 1159]

"All that is seen must die. Only God and his devotees are spiritually immortal." [SGGS 1100]

(This 'chance' pertains to the optimum and best utilization of this lifetime, for meditation, and for doing good unto others. One's own welfare would be a natural consequence, and a foregone conclusion).

First conquer the fear of death, learn to accept/embrace death; only then would you become worthy of living a pristinely sublime and selfless life. Humility and faith in God would result in fortitude.

"First, accept death, and give up any hope of life. Becoming the dust of the feet of all, and then, one may come to God. Accept that only one who has died, truly lives, and one who is alive, consider him dead. Those who are in love with the One Lord, are the blessed ones. Pain does not even approach that person, within whose mind God resides. Hunger and thirst do not affect him, and the messenger of death does not terrorize him." [SGGS 1102]

Whomsoever discovered this treasure-chest of Noumenon, his treasury shall overflow with piety, humility, prosperity and service.

Practicing what they preached, the Gurus and their worthy disciples demonstrated that human life is worthless if not lived with honor and dignity. The Fifth and the Ninth Gurus, along with all four sons of the 10th Guru, and innumerable brave ones sacrificed their lives, at the altar of religious fanaticism, in order to uphold and preserve the liberty to practice a faith of one's choice.

"In the beginning God created the heaven and the earth." (Genesis 1:1)

"This (the Sabbath) will be a sign between Me (God) and the Israelites forever, for in six days the Lord made heaven and earth, and on the seventh day He rested and was refreshed." (Exodus 31:17)

"When we (inhabitants of Jericho) heard [what the Israelites did to the Amorites Sihon and Og], our hearts melted. No courage remained in any inhabitant because of you, for the Lord, your God, He is God in heaven above, and on earth below." (Joshua 2:11)

"When the flame went up from atop the altar towards the Heavens, the angel of the Lord went up in the flame of the altar. Manoah and his wife watched and fell upon their faces to the ground." (Judges 13:20)

"They come from a far country, from the end of the heavens, Lord and His weapons of indignation, to destroy the whole land." (Isaiah 13:5)

"They will die horrible deaths; they will not be eulogized nor buried; they will be like dung upon the face of the earth. By the sword and by famine they will be consumed; their carcasses will be food for the birds of heaven and for the animals of the earth." (Jeremiah 16:4)

The existence of 'heaven' and/or 'hell', per se, has been denied by the Sikh Gurus. They reject outright the school of thought that these are some 'designated areas' where a soul is dispatched, as per commendable deeds, or misdeeds.

"Human ego ensnares one, thereby creating for the person 'heaven or hell'. Hankering after worldly pursuits, one creates hell for oneself." [SGGS 761]

"Wherever the saints reside, such a place reverberates with the ambience of heaven. They enshrine the lotus feet of God within their hearts. Listen, O mind and body, and recognize the way to find peace, so that you may eat and enjoy the various delicacies of the Lord. Taste the ambrosial nectar of the Naam, the Name of the Lord, within the mind. Its taste is wondrous — it cannot be described. All greed shall die, and all thirst shall be quenched. The humble beings seek the sanctuary of the supreme Lord God. The Lord dispels the fears and attachments of countless incarnations. God has showered His mercy and grace upon slave Nanak." [SGGS 1142]

"Creating the universe, God remains diffused throughout it. In the wind, water and fire, the Supreme is all pervasive. The waving mind seeks indulgence in evil passions and vices, forgetting its primal obligation towards the Creator. Forgetting God, one must be prepared to bear innumerable miseries. Consequently, such a misguided one suffers the ignominy of having to undergo 8.4 million reincarnations. This vicious cycle of death and rebirth has been termed as hell. Due to the present life misdeeds, one may be reborn as a four-legged animal, as a crawling serpent, as a flying bird, as a small insect or as a creature in wzater. In such dire straits, none from one's kith and kin shall be the savior; it is only within God power to rescue and redeem. Discard falsehood and attain the truth, and thus become the recipient of the rewards you desire. This, then, is the ideal and profitable bartering practice." [SGGS 1028]

"They said one to another: 'We are truly guilty concerning our brother, in that we saw the anguish of his soul, when he besought us, and we would not hear; therefore is this distress come upon us.'" (Genesis 42:21)

"On this day, I (God) will put the dread and fear of you (Israel) upon the nations that rest under the whole heaven; when they will hear the report of you, they will tremble and be in anguish because of you." (Deuteronomy 2)

"So, my loins became filled with anguish. Pains have taken hold of me, similar to a woman birth pangs; I was prostrated so I could not hear; I was saddened so that I could not see." (Isaiah 21)

"Nations tremble before it; all faces become covered with blackness." (Joel 2:6)

"When your fear arrives like a storm, and your calamity arrives like a stormy wind; when distress and anguish comes upon you." (Proverbs 1)

"When anguish arrives, they will seek out peace, but there shall be none." (Ezekiel 7)

"I heard a voice similar to a woman in labor, and the anguish of one who has her first child: the voice of Zion's daughter, sobbing and spreading out her hands, saying: 'Woe to me now. My soul faints before the killers.'" (Jeremiah 4)

"Inside me, my heart is in anguish and the horrors of death have fallen upon me." (Psalms 55)

"Burning and burning, writhing in pain, one wrings one's hands and goes insane. The Lord seems to be angry. The fault lies with the devotee, and not with the Lord. The devotee does not know His excellence and worth. Having wasted one's youth, now one comes to regret and repent." [SGGS 794]

"When the people of the world are suffering in pain, they call upon the Lord in loving prayer. The True Lord naturally listens and hears and gives comfort. He commands the God of rain, and the rain pours down in torrents. Corn and wealth are produced in great abundance and prosperity; their value cannot be estimated. Sayeth Nanak: Praise the Name of the Lord; He reaches out and sustains all beings. The mortal, never again, suffers in pain." [SGGS 1281]

In scientific-parlance, the 'rotations and revolutions' pertaining to the earth and the sun, bring about the change of seasons. It is a routine that is pre-programmed (in computer-jargon) in the characteristics of 'nature'. During scorching summers, the flow of rivers gets bogged down, while the same rivers become inundated during rainy season. They dry out in summers, and submerge the entire region when they flood. Vegetation cries out and birds and animals wail for a dewdrop and a raindrop, to quench their thirst. On hearing the pleas of the tormented souls, rains pour down, and flowers blossom, once again, and earth is rejuvenated.

Similarly, 'heat' is generated on the plane of the mind and soul, when desire, lust, anger, greed, attachment and other vices take their toll by vibrations and reverberations, attacking the human psyche. All the 'positives' have a cooling effect on the human mind and body. Compassion and contentment, forgiveness and morality, along with other qualities of the head and the heart, forge a powerful alliance to counter the armies of aggressive elements (vices). Soothing signals emanate from such calm souls, and both the sender and the receiver experience 'bliss'.

"Judah, you are the one who your brothers will praise. Your hand will be at your enemies' neck. Your father's children will prostrate before you." (Genesis 49)

"He (God) set you (Israel) high above all the nations that He made in praise, name, and in honor in order that you may be a holy people to the Lord, your God, as He has spoken." (Deuteronomy 26)

"I am the Lord; that is My Name. I will not tender My Glory to another, nor My praise to idols." (Isaiah 42)

"Draw me after you so that we may run; the king brought me into his chambers. We will be glad and rejoice in you; we will praise your love more than wine; unrestrained is there love for you." (Song of Songs 1:4)

Renounce both praise and criticism; seek, instead, the state of Nirvaana (salvation). Says Nanak: This is such a difficult game; only those with faith in God understand it! [SGGS 219]

"We have been burnt by the fires of the world. Some speak well of us, and some speak ill of us, but we have surrendered our body to God. Whoever comes to His sanctuary, is saved by His merciful grace. Humble Nanak has entered His sanctuary, Dear Lord, and pleads for the protection of his honor!" [SGGS 528]

"Even if one could live throughout the four ages, or even ten times more, and even if one were known throughout all the continents, and followed by all, with a good name and reputation, with praise and fame throughout the world—still, if the Lord does not bless one with His glance of grace, then who cares? What is the use? Among worms, one would be considered a lowly worm, and even contemptible sinners would hold one in contempt." [SGGS 2]

"It is not good to slander anyone, but the foolish, self-willed still do it. The faces of the slanderers are blackened, and they fall into the most horrible hell." [SGGS 755]

Praise is an intoxicant, but self-aggrandizement is a vice. When another praises one, the former is, naturally, on cloud nine. Ironically, one does not like some one else being praised. This is the characteristic of a jealous mind. Criticism hurts, and it hurts all the more when someone, having the ulterior motive of defaming another, criticizes a noble and praise worthy person. On the contrary, a sycophant (again, someone with a vested interest) would leave no stone unturned, to heap accolades and eulogies on an undeserving person.

"You will make holy garments for Aaron, your brother, [that will be both] for splendor and for beauty." (Exodus 28:2)

"For Aaron's sons, you will make tunics, girdles and turbans for splendor and for beauty." (Exodus 28:40)

"The beauty of Israel lie slain on your high places. How have the mighty fallen." (II Samuel 1:19)

"Babylon, the glory of kingdoms, the beauty of the Chaldeans' pride, will be again as when God overthrew Sodom and Gomorrah." (Isaiah 13)

"Your fame spread outward among the nations for your beauty, for it was perfect through My splendor that I granted you, says the Lord, God." (Ezekiel 16)

"So I will bring foreigners upon you, the most horrible of the nations. They will draw their swords against the beauty of your wisdom, and they will defile your brilliance (Ezekiel 28)

"The cedars in God's garden could not hide it. The cypress trees were not like its branches, and the plane trees were not like its boughs. Nor was any tree in God's garden was like it in its beauty." (Ezekiel 31)

"How great is His goodness, and how great is His beauty! Wheat will allow make the youthful to prosper, and fresh wine for the virgins." (Zachariah 9)

"Charisma is deceiving, and beauty is futile, but a woman who fears the Lord will be praised." (Proverbs 31)

"They alone are beautiful and attractive, who abide in the company of the holy. Those who have accumulated the wealth of the Lord's Name—they alone are wise investors, and are praised by all and sundry." [SGGS 132]

"Power is fraudulent, beauty is fraudulent, and wealth is fraudulent, as is pride of ancestry. Beholding the bitter melon, he is deceived, by appearance. But it is not worth even a shell; the illusionary riches will not go along with anyone." [SGGS 708]

"Beauty lies in the eyes of the beholder" is a realistically pertinent statement. And, equally true is the fact that beauty, besides being external and physical, is, also, internal, intellectual and spiritual. To admire the latter, the observer must be endowed with the 'third eye' having the potential of penetrating through bone and flesh, to have the heavenly-view of the inner-beauty of someone's heart and soul. A living personification of this statement is the crane, exquisitely adorable, but so deceitful, inside. But, the ugly looking nightingale, which has been blessed with the most mellifluous voice, churns out soothing music (even while it may be the regular language of the species). Some beautiful people are treacherous and wicked and cunning, while the so-described ugly ones are pious, learned and compassionate.

A child is showered with love and affection by all and sundry, owing to its qualities of beauty and innocence. It is free of the vices of greed, lust, malice, anger and ego. It is more carefree than the birds that fly in gay abandon. The child-like traits are visible in God's chosen few who continue to retain the charm and innocence, in word and spirit, until their last day. This Godly-attribute cannot be replenished and substituted by donning expensive ornaments and using cosmetics to look beautiful. Saints, seers, saviors and prophets, have a radiant gleam and glow on their faces, and a magnetic field and halo, around them, that would, instantaneously captivate anyone in range.

"God called the light 'day' and the darkness 'night.' There was evening and then morning: one day." (Genesis 1)

"Aaron acted accordingly; he lit its lamps to give light in front of the lamp, as the Lord had commanded Moses." (Numbers 8)

"The Lord said to Moses: 'Stretch out your hand toward the sky, and there will be darkness over Egypt: a darkness [so vivid] it could be felt.'" (Exodus 10)

"[God said to Moses:] 'Order the Israelites to bring to you pure oil for the light so that the lamp can continually burn.'" (Leviticus 24)

"When you (Moses) came close and stood aside the mountain, it burned with fire up the heights of heaven, along with darkness, clouds, and thick darkness [covering the mountain]." (Deuteronomy 4)

"Woe to those who call evil good or good evil, he who considers darkness to be light or light to be darkness, he who considers bitter to be sweet or sweet to be bitter." (Isaiah 5)

"David then arose along with all the people who were with him. They traveled across the Jordan, and by the time the sun rose, all of them had crossed the river." (II Samuel 17)

"I (King Belteshazzar) heard of you (Daniel), that the spirit of the gods is within you, that the clarity of understanding and excellent wisdom are all found in you." (Daniel 5:14)

"The Guru has provided the healing ointment of spiritual wisdom, and dispelled the darkness of ignorance. By the Lord's grace, one meets the saint. Sayeth Nanak: My mind has been enlightened." [SGGS 293]

"If a hundred moons were to rise, and a thousand suns appeared, even with such light, there would still be terrifying darkness (in the mind), without the Guru's guidance. Says Nanak: Those who do not think of the Guru, and who think of themselves as clever, shall be left abandoned in the field, like the scattered sesame." [SGGS 463]

Darkness can be found all over, in great measure within man's mind, and without. The earth's crust is dark towards the interior. The deeper levels of the oceans are dark, the sun's light being unable to permeate beyond a specified range (fathoms). Due to the increased effect of the vices of lust, greed, egocentricism, hatred, jealousy, violence and addictions, even more darkness can be found within the hearts, minds and souls of modern man.

The germs of disease originate in dark regions. Snakes and scorpions are often found in dark areas. Dacoits and marauders wait for their prey in dark and nether confines. So do the lowly vices wait for the opportune moment to launch a vicious attack targeted towards persons with a weak power of resilience. 'Darkness' is a synonym for 'sorrow', 'grief' and 'penury'. Ostentatious illuminations and fireworks are on display during festivities and rejoicing. Due to the darkness of ignorance, coupled with a lack of will and interest, to search and pray for the true light, today's man is lost and frightened. Finding oneself in deep peril, there seems to be no happiness, notwithstanding the rapid strides towards the destinations of acquiring material wealth and accruing knowledge.

"The Lord gave Solomon wisdom, as He had promised him. There was peace between Hiram and Solomon as the two had forged a covenant together." (I Kings 5)

The Talmud has a great example to illustrate the idea of 'pious foolishness'. It asks: "Would you like to know who is a pious fool?" It is a man standing by the seashore, wrapped in his '*tallit*', devoutly engrossed in prayer. (A '*tallit'* is the prayer shawl with fringes on its four corners). Suddenly, he hears screams from a drowning person, crying and pleading to be saved. Knowing well that he could save the person, he continues to stand his ground, refusing to forsake God, with whom he is presently in conversation with, just in order to save a mere mortal in distress. The rabbis call such a person a 'pious fool', the religious and politest way of calling him an 'undeniable idiot'.

"One of them told David: 'Ahithophel is one of the conspirators with Absalom.' David responded: 'Lord, I beseech you: turn Ahithophel's council to foolishness.'" (II Samuel 15)

"You (Moses) must speak to all who are wise hearted, to those who I (God) have filled with the spirit of wisdom so that they will make Aaron's garments to consecrate him, so that he may serve Me in the capacity of being a priest." (Exodus 28)

"May sure to keep them (the commandments), for they are your (Israelites) wisdom and your understanding in the nation's view. For when they will hear all these statutes, they will say: 'Surely this great nation is a wise and understanding people.'" (Deuteronomy 4)

"Joshua, the son of Nun, was full of the spirit of wisdom, for Moses had pressed his hands upon him. The Israelites listened to him and acted as the Lord had commanded Moses." (Deuteronomy 34)

"A person performing a misdeed, fully well aware and conscious of the repercussions, thereof, and realizing the fallout, is deemed to be the greatest fool. Instead of feeling guilt or remorse, he becomes arrogant and egocentric, and takes pride in his actions. He is like the one who falls into a well, despite carrying a glowing lamp, with him." [SGGS 1376]

God gave humans the unique gift of the power of analysis, and by the optimum utilization of the nervous system (the brain), one could achieve wonders. But, rarely, does that happen. A child's thinking faculties are not fully developed, hence cannot be called a fool. But, such an adult is a fool, who does not think and act rationally. A person lacking in wisdom, does not act in consonance with certain universally acclaimed and socially acceptable norms.

A literate or educated person may not, necessarily, be a wise one, too. But, God may gift an illiterate person with the blessing of wisdom. And while there's no guarantee that an educated person would realize God, there have been great devotees who never learnt the Three "Rs" in school, but mastered the highest techniques of Communion with God. Another myth and ill conceived notion pertains to the prevalent practice of linking intelligence and wisdom with wealth and prestige. A person who is successful in a given vocation/profession might not, necessarily, be considered wise in other spheres, too. Generally, there is a tendency to become dependant upon such people in various matters, including spiritual-religious and socio-economic, even though the concerned person might not be, remotely, having an affinity with the said issues.

"To woman (Eve), He (God) said: 'I will compound the pain experienced during child birth: in distress you will bring forth children. Also, you will desire your husband, and he will rule over you.'" (Genesis 3)

"Look at joy and happiness: people are slaying bulls, killing sheep, consuming meat and imbibing wine; let us eat and drink, for tomorrow we die." (Isaiah 22)

"The nations will hear [what the Israelites experienced] and be afraid. Distress will take hold of the Philistines." (Exodus 15)

"The Jews experienced light, gladness, joy and honor." (Esther 8)

"I (God) also will do this to you (Israelites); I will appoint over you terror, consumption and fever, that will consume the eyes, and cause distress to the heart. You will sow your fields in vain as your enemies will consume the harvest." (Leviticus 26)

"Deception is in the heart of those who plan to do evil, but the advisors of peace enjoy happiness." (Proverbs 12)

"You (Israelites) will not find any peace among these nations, nor will your foot's sole find serenity. The Lord will show you a frightened heart, failing of eyes and sadness of mind." (Deuteronomy 28)

"While My (God) servants will sing at of happiness, you will sob out of sadness and will scream because of your troubled spirit." (Isaiah 65)

"The they will arrive and sing in the height of Zion. The Lord's goodness will flow like corn, wine and oil, for the children of the flock and the herd. Their soul will be similar to a watered garden, but they will not sulk in sorrow any longer." (Jeremiah 31)

"One who understands the essence of a 'life-Divine', such a humble one (ever in God's servitude) is very rare. He has, not even, an iota of pain, and is, totally, at peace. There is no defeat — he is totally victorious. He is never in sorrow — he is happy, always. Says Nanak: The humble servant of the Lord is himself the Lord (becomes identical; resembles godly-attributes); he does not come and go in the vicious cycle of reincarnation." [SGGS 1302]

Sorrow and pain is like an epidemic, the only cure for it being the regular administering of dosages of Noumenon of God. None has escaped the octopus-like tentacles of sorrow. Since the desires are innumerable, the causes of sorrow are countless, too. When desires are not fulfilled, pain is born, therefrom.

"In hope, there is very great pain; the self-willed focuses his consciousness on it. The God-loving become desire less, and attain supreme peace. In the midst of their household, they remain detached; Sorrow and separation do not cling to them at all. They are pleased with the Lord's will. Says Nanak: They remain forever immersed in the primal Lord, who blends them with Himself." [SGGS 1249]

It is human nature to be jealous of another's happiness, and to cry hoarsely at one's sorrow. But, in reality, none is actually happy, in this world. The nodal point and focus of all happiness (the reservoir of joy and bliss) is God and meditation on His Name. Every laugh is attached with the apprehension of a wail looming large. And behind the curtain of all praise and accolades, lurks the dangerous snake of exposure, insult and defamation. Profits are, naturally, made at great stakes and risks. Hence, all efforts should be made to decorate this life with all worthy attributes and ornamentation, so as to be received by God, in His magnificent kingdom, with honor and praise. At that moment, disgrace and rebuke can be avoided, if one had the wisdom, of doing so, during the time that was available, for meditation.

"Because of this I (God) will hand over their wives to others, their fields to those others who will start to bequeath them. Every one from the slightest to the mightiest acts greedily. From the prophet to the priest, they all act treacherously." (Jeremiah 8)

"You who live near many waters, rich with treasures, your close has come to your vast greed." (Jeremiah 51)

"As his greed could not fathom an end, he will not preserve anything of that which he desired." (Job 20)

"What good is food, and what good are attires & adornments, if the True Lord does not abide within the mind? What good are fruits, what good is butter, what good is sweet molasses, and what good is flour? What good are clothes, and what good is a soft bed, to enjoy pleasures and sensual delights? What good is an army, and what good are soldiers, servants and mansions to live in? Says Nanak: Without the True Name, all this paraphernalia is perishable." [SGGS 142]

"Nanak wonders: What has happened to the world? There is no guide or friend. There is no love, even among brothers and relatives. For the sake of worldly riches, people have lost their faith. They weep and wail. They slap their faces and pull their hair out. But if they chant the Name of the Lord, they shall be absorbed into it." [SGGS 1410]

Greed is considered to be a major vice that leads one onto other dangerous vices like violence and deceit. It assumes the proportions of a mental disease, when in reaches the saturation point.

The natural equilibrium is disturbed when a greedy person accumulates immense wealth while another person has to shiver in the cold, without shelter, sans clothing.

To remain happy with whatsoever one has, is 'true contentment'. This should not be misconstrued to imply that being ambitious is negative, provided the rapid strides towards success do not in any way impinge upon another's interests. Abundance of wealth and materials does not guarantee happiness. Peace is the direct consequence of contentment. Being progressive is welcome, without usurping another's rights and privileges.

"Whoever illegally has relations with an unredeemed slave girl betrothed to another, and freedom has not been given to her, there will be an inquiry, but she should not be put to death as she was never freed." (Leviticus 19:20)

"They (Egyptians) made their (Israelites) lives tough with hard labor, mortar, brick and in all kinds of service of the field. Whatever they were made to do, was made to be exceptionally burdensome." (Exodus 1:14)

"I am the Lord, your God, who delivered you (Israelites) from the land of Egypt, from the house of slavery." (Deuteronomy 5)

"The Lord, our God, delivered us (Israelites) and our forefathers from the land of Egypt, from the house of slavery. He made great signs in front of us, and preserved us wherever we traveled, through all the nations through which we traveled." (Joshua 24)

"The Lord sent a prophet to the Israelites. H said to them: 'The Lord, God of Israel, said: 'I delivered you from Egypt, and delivered you from the house of slavery.'" (Judges 6)

"When the Lord allows you (Israelites) to rest from your distress, from your anxiety and from the hard slavery which you were made to do." (Isaiah 14)

"I (God) delivered you (Israelites) from the land of Egypt, and redeemed you from the house of slavery. I sent before you Moses, Aaron and Miriam." (Micah 6)

"Now, the Merciful Lord hath decreed that nobody shall persecute and torture another, and that all may reside in peace and harmony, under His Benevolent Rule." [SGGS 74]

"Fareed implores the Lord, not to let him live on alms, and on another's mercy. Instead, he would prefer death, to slavery." [SGGS 1380]

"The battle-drums and conch-shells signal the commencement of the battle. The spiritual warriors enter the battlefield, in all their paraphernalia and regalia. He alone is known as a spiritual hero, who fights in defense of religion (not the religions or faiths that we have founded, but the religion of the Lord: that wants us to sacrifice our lives for peace and justice, and to never let cowardice devour us). He may be cut apart, limb by limb, but he never withdraws from the war-zone." [SGGS 1105]

The God-loving and the God-fearing warriors would never subjugate another, but would use their power to protect the weak and the downtrodden, the oppressed and the suppressed. Freedom is the birthright of every human, while slavery is a curse. In this context, it is noteworthy that the Sikh people have been relentlessly carrying on an agitation, demanding a separate homeland, as promised by the lawmakers of free India at the time of framing the Constitution of India, at the end of the imperialistic colonial rule of the British, who created Pakistan, on religious lines, as an Islamic State.

Most recently, since 1984 when the Indian regime launched a warlike operation to attack the holiest Sikh shrine, The Golden Temple, the Sikhs have been constantly persecuted, dubbed as extremists, killed in fake police and army encounters, and jailed without free-trial, for several years. The Sikhs have been waging a struggle for freedom, due to the Spirit of Freedom that was inculcated in them by all Gurus.

Section 4

****

CAUTION

****

"The companionship of hypocrites will be dismal and fire will consume the tents of bribery." (Job 15)

"You may not give God's bread to a stranger's hand because their corruption and blemishes are in them; they may not be accepted by you." (Leviticus 22)

"Corruption does not belong to Him (God) but to Him children who are blemished (Israelites); they are a contrarian and crooked generation." (Deuteronomy 32)

"The altars located in Jerusalem, on the right of the Mount of Corruption, Solomon, the king of Israel, built for Ashtoreth the abomination of the Sidonians, and for Kemosh the abomination of the Moabites, and for Milcom the abomination of the Ammonites, the king defiled." (II Kings 23)

"The self-willed egoistic persons read and study, but they do not know the way. They do not understand the Name of the Lord; they wander, deluded and deluged by doubt. They take bribes, and give false testimony; the noose of evil-mindedness is around their necks, and they shall hang themselves. They read the Scriptures; they argue and debate, but do not know the essence of reality; they indulge in rituals and ceremonial practices. Without the perfect Guru, the essence of reality is not obtained. The true and pure beings walk the path of Truth. He Himself is wise, and He Himself judges the Truth. Those whom God blesses with His glance of grace become God-loving, and praise the word of the holy hymns." [SGGS 1032]

Such actions and deeds are severely deplorable and tantamount to a grave sin. Feeding one's children from the money gotten through corrupt means, is just like poisoning their food with the venom of a snake. A person whose intake is such, shall have vitriolic speech and a foul tongue, never pleasant in conversation and in his dealings with others.

Such misdemeanors of the corrupt do not go unpunished. They shall be penalized, on earth, and in God's Supreme Court.

CRUELTY

"Simon and Levi are brothers; their swords are instruments of cruelty." (Genesis 49)

"The cruelty done to Jerubaal's seventy sons will come, and their blood will be upon Avimelech, their brother." (Judges 9)

"You have not strengthened the weak, nor have you healed the sick, nor have you fixed the broken, nor have you returned that which was driven away, nor have you searched out that which was lost. Rather, with compulsion and malice you ruled them." (Ezekiel 34)

"Look at the covenant as the earth's dark places are full of the world's cruelty." (Psalms 74)

"One has not forsaken sexual desire, and not forgotten anger; greed has not departed, either. There's no stop to slandering and gossiping about others. All service is useless and fruitless. By breaking into the houses of others and robbing them, one fills one's belly, what a sinner. But, when this sinner goes to the world beyond, he shall be notorious, for all his acts of omission and commission, that he hath committed, due to ignorance. Cruelty has not left his mind; he has not cherished kindness for other living beings." [SGGS 1253]

"When oppression and tyranny are on the ascendant, a myriad array of vices controls the human-frame (body and mind). The bondage of self-aggrandizement can be gotten rid of by meditating upon God's Name. That's the only remedy for the tormented oppressor as well as the weak and cowardly oppressed." [SGGS 255]

"The emperor who struck down the poor, has been burnt in the fire by the supreme Lord God. The Creator administers true justice. He is the saving grace of His slaves." [SGGS 199]

"It is tyranny to use force; the Lord shall call the cruel to account. And then they shall be tortured and humiliated, in the Lord's court. Keep the slate of conscience clean and clear, to become the recipient of God's grace. Only then, in the true court of the Lord, one shall not be captured or put in shackles. [SGGS 1375]

"I (God) will place enmity between you and woman, and between your seed and her seed. It will bruise your head and you will injure his heel." (Genesis 3)

"Both the days of punishment and reward have arrived. Israel will know it. While the prophet is foolish, the man of the spirit is crazy because of the vastness of your sins and the great abhorrence." (Hosea 9)

"The Lord, God, said: 'Since the Philistines have acted vengefully with an angry soul to destroy it eternally in hatred.'" (Ezekiel 25)

"The Lord, your (Israelites) God, is a jealous God with you. Do not allow the anger of the Lord, your God, to flare against you and wipe you off the face of the earth." (Deuteronomy. 6)

"Or if in hatred he strikes him with his hand fatally, the striker will be put to death, for he is a murderer. The avenger of blood may execute the murderer when he meets him." (Numbers 35)

"The Lord will not spare him, but rather the anger of the Lord and His jealousy shall flare against that man, and all the curses that are written in this book will be placed upon him. The Lord will blot out his name from under the heavens." (Deuteronomy 29)

"They (Israelites) caused Me (God) to act jealousy with them; they provoked Me to act angrily with their vanities. I will cause them to act jealousy with others; I will cause them to act angrily with a foolish nation." (Deuteronomy 32)

"Neither their silver nor their gold will help them on the day of the Lord's wrath. Instead, the whole world will be consumed by the fire of his jealousy. He (God) will make an end, a sudden end, of all those living in the land." (Zephaniah 1)

"Do not harbor hatred against anyone. In each and every heart, God is contained. The all-pervading Lord is permeating and pervading the oceans and the land. How rare are those who, by Guru's grace, sing of Him. Hatred and alienation depart from those who, as devotees, listen to the hymns of the Lord's praises. Says Nanak: One who becomes a devotee chants the Name of the Lord, and rises above all social classes and status symbols. Acting in egotism, selfishness and conceit, the foolish, ignorant, faithless cynic wastes his life. He dies in agony, like one dying of thirst." [SGGS 259]

"To some, the Lord has given silks and satins, and to some, beds decorated with cotton ribbons. Some do not even have a poor patched coat, and some live in thatched huts. Do not indulge in envy and bickering, O my mind. By continually performing good deeds, O my mind, you may have the luxuries, but not through jealousy. The potter works with the same clay, and colors the pots in different ways. Into some, he sets pearls (of contentment and compassion), while to others, he attaches filth (of hatred, and an envious nature)." [SGGS 479]

Harboring animosity towards our fellow human beings is tantamount to perpetrating violence on our own soul. It's like raising a banner of revolt against God and his offspring. And, as all of us are His children, it is inferred that its equivalent to fighting with our own siblings, rebelling against our own kith and kin.

"A prayer of David: Hear the right Lord, heed my cry; give ear to my prayer from these lips which are free of deceit." (Psalms 17)

"One who acts with deceit will not dwell in My (God's) house. One who tells lies will not stay in My sight." (Psalms 101)

"The acumen of the cautious is to contemplate His (God's) way, but the idiocy of the stupid is deceitfulness." (Proverbs14)

"My lips will not utter speak iniquity, nor will my tongue speak with deceitfulness." (Job 27)

"Your prophets have perceived futile and silly visualizations for you. They did not expose your iniquity, to restore your captivity, but have prophesied for you burdens of lies and deceitfulness." (Lamentations 2)

"And through his intelligence, he will make deceitfulness beneficial under his watch. He will enlarge himself in his heart, and without complexity will annihilate multitudes. He will also stand against the prince of princes, but he will not be broken by any human hand." (Daniel 8)

"'Your world lies in the midst of deceitfulness. Only because of lies do they refuse to know me,' says the Lord." (Jeremiah 9)

"Ephraim enclosed me with prevarications, and the house of Israel with deceit. But, Judah still rules with God and is faithful with the holy ones." (Hosea 12)

"Accordingly, you will give presents to Moresheth-Gath. The houses of Achzib will be a lie to the kings of Israel." (Micah 1)

The mortal does not remember the Lord; he wanders around, engrossed in greed. Committing sins, he dies, and his life ends in an instant. His body is like a clay vessel or a brittle metal pot. If you wish to keep it safe and sound, then meditate on the Lord; Chant the Name of the Lord. Chanting His Name night and day, the Lord will eventually hear your call. Says Kabeer: The body is a banana forest, and the mind is an intoxicated elephant. The jewel of spiritual wisdom is the prod, and the rare Saint is the rider. [1376 SGGS]

"He commits innumerable robberies, countless acts of adultery, millions of falsehoods and thousands of abuses. He practices infinite number of deceptions and secret deeds, night and day, against his fellow beings." [SGGS 471]

When man tries to think of fooling others by being a master-trickster, he too, shall someday become an unsuspecting victim of his own game plan. He is sure to have a taste of his own bitter potion.

"Fire and water join together, and the breath roars in its fury! The tongue and the sex organs each seek to taste. The eyes which look upon corruption do not know the love and the fear of God. Conquering self-conceit, one obtains the Name. One who dies (immerses) oneself in the Word of the Lord, shall never again have to die. Without such a death, how can one attain perfection? The mind is engrossed in deception, treachery and duality. Whatever the Immortal Lord does, comes to pass." [SGGS 153]

"The righteous one will rejoice when he sees the vengeance; he will be able to cleanse his feet with the blood of the evildoer." (Psalms 58)

"Lord, God, vengeance belongs to You; God, vengeance belongs to You so shine forth." (Psalms 94)

"Jealousy is man's anger; he will not be able to be spared on the day of vengeance." (Proverbs 6)

"You have observed all their vengeance and all their schemes against me." (Lamentations 3)

"Whether constructing an altar to reject the Lord, or to use it to offer burnt, meal offerings, or peace offerings on it, let the Lord Himself take vengeance." (Joshua 22)

"She said to him: 'My father: if you have spoken to the Lord, act to me according to that which has come from your mouth, considering that the Lord has taken vengeance for you of your enemies, on the Ammonites.'" (Judges 11)

"This is the Lord's day of vengeance, and the year of recompenses for Zion's cause." (Isaiah 34)

"But, Lord of hosts, as you judge righteously and test one's innermost feeling, allow me to witness your vengeance on them, for I have revealed my cause." (Jeremiah 11)

"The Lord, God, said: 'Edom revolted against the House of Judah by taking vengeance, and has greatly offended and revenged himself upon them.'" (Ezekiel 25)

"I will execute vengeance in anger and rage upon the nations, such as they have never heard." (Micah 5)

"Answer evil with goodness; do not fill the mind with anger, thus your body shall not suffer from any disease, and one shall obtain everything. Says Fareed: The bird (human-being) is a guest in this beautiful world-garden. The morning drums are beating, indicating it is, now, time for departure (moment of death). Musk is distributed during the night; those in deep slumber shall never become the recipients of their share of this Blessed commodity (hence do not harbor any ill-will towards another, during this short span of a 'night', that is this lifetime)." [SGGS 1381]

"Do not turn around and strike those who strike you with their fists. Kiss their feet, and return to your own home (do not generate a feeling of remorseful revenge, as it is harmful for your progress). When there was time to earn name and fame, by performing worthy deeds, one was in love with the world, instead." [SGGS 1378]

"Do not harbor evil intentions against others, and by so doing one shall not be troubled. The Name of the Lord, as preached by the True Guru, is the effective mendicant, and not the Tantric-rituals or the Mantra-recitations or the Yogic-postures. Nanak experiences this peace night and day." [SGGS 386]

"If you (Cain) act appropriately, shall your repentance not be accepted? And if you do not act appropriately, sin lies at your doorstep. To you will be his desire, but you may rule over him."(Genesis 4)

"Every day, you must offer a bull as a sin offering for atonement. You must clean the altar, and when you have made an atonement for it, you will anoint it in order to sanctify it." (Exodus 29)

"He should press his hands upon the head of the sin offering, and offer the sin offering in the place of the burnt offering." (Leviticus 4)

"Aaron should bring the sin offering bull for himself; it should be an atonement for himself and for his house. He should kill the sin offering bull for himself." (Leviticus 16)

"The priest should bring them before the Lord and offer his sin and burnt offering." (Numbers 6)

"If a man done a sin warranting the death penalty, then you should out him to death, and then hang him from on a tree." (Deuteronomy 21)

"Fathers should not be executed for the sins of their children, nor should the children be put to death on account of their fathers. Every person should die only for his own sin." (Deuteronomy 24)

"And for me, God forbid me to stop praying for you as it would be a sin against the Lord. But, I will teach you the good and the right path." (I Samuel 12)

"Take heed in heaven and forgive your people Israel's sin. Return them again to the land that You gave to their fathers." (I Kings 8)

"Virtue and sin exist in the body together." [SGGS 126]

"O kind father, ignore my sins." [SGGS 12]

"The sinners act, and perform nefarious acts (misdeeds), and then they weep and wail, when such acts misfire and backfire. Says Nanak: just as the churning stick churns the butter, so does the judge of righteousness torture them. Says Nanak: Speaking in righteousness, one's world (home) becomes sanctified." [SGGS 1425]

"Emulate the one who binds in bondage his evil and corrupted gaze. One who does not know the difference between vice and virtue wanders around uselessly, and aimlessly." [SGGS 1329]

Due to ignorance, egotism and lust for power, sex and wealth, man has sacrificed man at the altar of his multifarious cravings. The height of inhumanity was when man did not think twice before sacrificing fellow-beings, to appease God. Now, this is an absurd and ridiculous level, to which man stooped. How could God, the Father and Mother, be asking for the sacrifice of one child, to be perpetrated by another. The same feeble argument (appeasement of God) has been repeatedly advanced regarding man enslaving man over the centuries, and for retaining extra-judicial control over others' land, life and family members. Inhuman and undignified behavior was evident when man forced women to marry several husbands, at any given point in time, and when man had a 'harem' comprised of hundreds of ladies for the satisfaction of his carnal-instincts. Religious intolerance was at its pinnacle, but the fanatic was considered to be the most pious one. Discrimination, on account of race, gender, color, creed, status, caste and religion, have been the other indelible black spots on the canvas. All such thoughts, words and deeds that are detrimental or prejudicial to the interests of another, are tantamount to being a "sin". Quite often, a sin may be an act of omission, rather than that of commission.

"Like a wife who commits adultery, who procures strangers instead of her husband." (Ezekiel 16)

"Will you (Israelites) steal, murder, commit adultery, swear falsely, burn incense to Baal, and walk after other gods that you do not know?" (Jeremiah 7)

"There is swearing, lying, killing, stealing, and committing adultery; they break all bounds and blood leads to blood." (Hosea 4)

"Whoever commits adultery with a woman is lacking in understanding; one who commits such an act destroys his own life." (Proverbs 6)

"Do not commit adultery." (Exodus 20)

"The man who commits adultery with another man's wife, the adulterer and the adulteress should be executed." (Leviticus 20)

ADULTERY

"Overflowing with sexual desire, one's intellect is stained with darkness; in the heat of youthful passion, one looks with desire upon the faces of other men's wives, unable to distinguish between good and evil. Drunk with sexual desire and other great sins, one goes astray, and does not distinguish between vice and virtue." [SGGS 93]

"Others' spouses, others' wealth, greed, egotism, corruption, evil passions, slander of others, sexual desire and anger — all of these are like venom; give up all these." [SGGS 1255]

"The Lord, God, made every tree grow out of the ground that is pleasant to the eyes and good for food. The tree of life was in the center of the garden along with the tree of knowledge of good and evil." (Genesis 2)

"God saw that man's evilness was pervasive on the earth and that all of his imagination and thoughts of his heart were only evil continually." (Genesis 6)

"The Lord passed by before him (Moses) and proclaimed: 'Lord, Lord, God, merciful and gracious, long suffering, and abundant in goodness and truth.'" (Exodus 34)

"The Lord will extricate from you (Israelites) all sickness, and will not place any of the evil diseases that He placed upon Egypt upon you. Rather, He will place them upon all those who hate you." (Deuteronomy 7)

"For seven days and nights, they sat down with him (Job) on the ground. No one spoke to him at all, for they saw the intensity of his suffering." (Job 2)

"When it happens that all good things have come upon you which the Lord, your God, promised you. The Lord will also bring upon you all evil things, until he has annihilated you from off this good land, which the Lord, your God, has given you." (Joshua 23)

"Lord, You know. Remember and be aware of me. Take revenge for me on my persecutors. Do not take me away in your long suffering. Know that for Your sake I have suffered insult." (Jeremiah 15)

"When they (Jacob's sons) left the city, but were not quite far off yet, Joseph said to his steward: 'Get up, follow after the men and when you

"God, the world is burning in its own sins. Save it through your mercy." [SGGS 853]

The 'demonic evil' manifests itself in negative thoughts, harsh words and cruel deeds, perpetrated against one another, consequently bringing great suffering for both (oppressor and oppressed) in the long run.

"The pain of separation is as unbearable as the pain of extreme hunger. The greatest, and unendurable, pain is the attack of the messenger of death. Another pain is the disease consuming my body. O doctor, don't administer the medicine. The pain persists, and the body continues to suffer. This medicine has no effect. Forgetting his Lord and Master, the mortal enjoys sensual pleasures; then, disease wells up in his body. The blind (ignorant/foolish) mortal receives his punishment. The value of sandalwood lies in its fragrance. The value of a human lasts only as long as the breath in the body. When the breath is taken away, the body crumbles into dust. The mortal's body emanates a golden-aura, and the soul-swan is immaculate and pure, if even a tiny particle of the Immaculate Name resides within. Only then shall all pain and disease be eradicated. Says Nanak: The mortal is saved through the True Name." [SGGS 1256]

"Worldly possessions are obtained by pain and suffering; when they are gone, they leave pain and suffering. Says Nanak: Without the True Name, hunger is never satisfied. Beauty does not satisfy hunger; when the man sees beauty, he hungers even more. As many as are the pleasures of the body, so many are the pains, which afflict it." [SGGS 1287]

"Because you said: 'We made a covenant with death; with the underworld, we made an agreement; when the overflowing scourge will pass through, it will not come to us, for we have made lies our refuge and under falsehood we hid ourselves.'" (Isaiah 28)

"Against whom do you make game? Against whom do you open your mouth wide, and pull out the tongue? Are you not children of transgression, a seed of falsehood?" (Isaiah 57)

"When you transgress and lie against the Lord, departing away from our God, speaking of oppression and revolt, conceiving and uttering words of falsehood from the heart." (Isaiah 59)

"Every person becomes a fool without knowledge; every goldsmith is shamed by his idols, for his molten image is falsehood, and there is no life in them." (Jeremiah 10)

"'This is your ration, the portion I set for you,' said the Lord. You forgot me and trusted in falsehood." (Jeremiah 13)

"Every man becomes stupid without knowledge; every goldsmith is put to shame by the carved idol; for his molten image is falsehood, and there is no breath in them." (Jeremiah 51)

"When I healed Israel, the sin of Ephraim was uncovered as well as the wickedness of Samaria, for they commit falsehood. The thief enters and the bandits steal outside." (Hosea 7)

"If a man who moves in hot air and falsehood would lie saying: 'I will lecture to you regarding wine and strong drink, even he would be the lecturer of this people!'" (Micah 2)

"When mouths speak of vanity, their right hand is a right hand of falsehood." (Psalms 144)

"Through the Guru's Teachings, some eliminate selfishness and conceit, and meditate on the Name of the Lord. Undertaking any other task, they waste their lives in vain. Without the Name, all that they wear and eat is poison. Praising Him, they merge with the True Lord. Investing counterfeit capital, they earn only falsehood in the world." [SGGS 144]

"Falsehood and corruption cause terrible suffering. All the religious robes and social classes look just like dust. Whoever is born, continues to come and go. O Nanak, only the Naam and the Lord's Command are eternal and everlasting." [SGGS 352]

"The intellect of the self-willed is engrossed in falsehood. Without the meditative remembrance of the Lord, it suffers in sin. Renounce evil-mindedness, and you shall reap the rewards. Whoever is born, comes through the unknowable and mysterious Lord." [SGGS 356]

"The self-willed practices falsehood, only falsehood. He never attains the mansion of the Lord presence. Attached to duality, he wanders, deluded by doubt. Entangled in worldly attachments, he comes and goes. Behold, the decorations of the discarded bride! Her consciousness is attached to children, spouse, wealth, and Maya, falsehood, emotional attachment, hypocrisy and corruption." [SGGS 363]

"Sin is bad, but it is dear to the sinner. He loads himself with sin, and expands his world through sin. Sin is far away from one who understands himself. He is not afflicted by sorrow or separation. Falsehood is bad, and death is cruel. The mind is enveloped by entanglements, and into entanglements it falls. Without the Name, how can anyone be saved? They rot away in sin." [SGGS 935]

"God said to Noah: 'The end of all flesh has come before Me, as the earth is filled with violence because of them. I will destroy them along with the earth.'" (Genesis 6)

"If one sins against the Lord, and lies to his friend regarding a matter that he was supposed to safeguard, or watch through partnership, or regarding an object taken away through violence…" (Leviticus 5)

"The God is my rock and in Him I trust. He is my shield, the horn of my salvation, my high tower, my refuge and my Savior who saves me from violence." (II Samuel 22)

"Their webs will not become garments, nor will they cover themselves with their works. Their works are of iniquity and the act of violence is in their hands." (Isaiah 59)

"Whenever I speak, I wail out loud. I shout of the issues of violence and ruin. The Lord's word is like a criticism of me and a ridicule all day long." (Jeremiah 20)

"Violence has climbed up like a staff of wickedness; none of them will remain, nor their abundance, nor their splendor, nor will be there any crying for them." (Ezekiel 7)

"Egypt will be desolate and Edom will be a wilderness - for the violence perpetrated against the people of Judah - because they shed innocent blood in their land." (Joel 4)

"'They lack the cognizance to act rightly,' the Lord said. '[This includes] those who stockpile violence and robbery in their palaces." (Amos 3)

"Because you acted violently against your brother Jacob, shame will be your lot, and you will be cut off forever." (Obadiah 1)

"Holy saints, this mind cannot be restrained. Fickle desires dwell with it, and so it cannot remain steady. The heart is filled with anger and violence, which cause all sense to be forgotten. The jewel of spiritual wisdom has been taken away from everyone; nothing can withstand it." [SGGS 219]

"Listen, O my friends: let's join together and make an effort to surrender to our Husband Lord. Renouncing our pride, let's charm Him with the potion of devotional worship, and the mantra of the holy saints. O my companions, when He comes under our power, He shall never leave us again. This is the good nature of the Lord God. O Nanak, God dispels the fear of old age, death and hell; He purifies His beings. Listen to my sincere prayer: let's make this firm resolve. In the peaceful poise of intuitive bliss, violence will be gone, as we sing the glorious praises of the Lord of the universe. Our pains and troubles shall be eradicated, and our doubts shall be dispelled; we will receive the fruits of our minds' desires. O Nanak, meditate on the Naam, the Name of the supreme Lord God, the perfect, transcendent Lord." [SGGS 249]

"My beloved Lord God is not far away. My mind is pleased and appeased by the word of the True Guru's teachings. I have found the Lord, the support of my breath of life. This is the way to meet your Husband Lord. Blessed is the soul-bride who is loved by her Husband Lord. Social class and status, race, ancestry and skepticism are eliminated, following the Guru's Teachings and contemplating the word. One whose mind is pleased and appeased, has no egotistical pride. Violence and greed are forgotten. The soul-bride intuitively ravishes and enjoys her Husband Lord; as Guru's chosen one, she is embellished by His Love." [SGGS 93]

"The enemy said: 'I will pursue, overtake and divide the plunder. My lust will be quenched through them. I will draw my sword and my hand will annihilate them." (Exodus 15)

"A wild ass is accustomed to the desert, sniffing the wind in its desire. In its lust, who can turn it away? Any one who seeks it out need not weary themselves. In its month, they will find it." (Jeremiah 2)

"She did not stop from engaging in harlotry sent from Egypt. In her early years, they lay with her and were able to handle her youthful body and poured out their lust upon her." (Ezekiel 23)

"The Babylonians came to her in the bed of love. They defiled her with their lust and she became polluted because of them. Her soul turned away from them.' (Ezekiel 23)

"They could not be sated with their lust, as their food still occupies their mouths." (Psalms 78)

"Do not lust after her beauty in your heart, nor allow her to take you away with her eyelids." (Proverbs 6)

"The righteousness of the honest will save them, but transgressors will be caught by their own lust." (Proverbs 11)

"Beauty and sexual desire are friends; hunger and tasty food are tied together. Greed is bound up in its search for wealth, and sleep will use even a tiny space as a bed. Anger barks and brings ruin on itself, blindly pursuing useless conflicts. It is good to be silent, because without the Name of the Lord, one's mouth spews forth only filth. Royal power, wealth, beauty, social status and youth are the five thieves. These thieves have plundered the world; no one's honor has been spared. But these thieves themselves are robbed, by those who fall at the Guru's feet." [SGGS 1288]

"O Lord and Master, in ignorance this mind is sold out, and is, now, in Illusion's hands. Lord and Master, the Guru of the World, here's a lustful being of the Dark Iron-Age (KaliYuga). The five vices have corrupted the mind. Moment by moment, they lead the mind further away from the Lord." [SGGS 710]

Unbridled sexual indulgence and promiscuity have been the sole cause of the spread of the deadly epidemic called AIDS, along with several other life-endangering diseases.

Judaism *ANGER IS DEMONIC*

"The Lord's anger was kindled against Moses; He said: 'Is not Aaron, the Levite, your brother? I know that he can speak well. So, when he comes to meet you and sees you, he will be happy in his heart.'" (Exodus 4)

"Jacob was anger with Rachel. He said: 'Am I in God's stead who can withhold children from you?'" (Genesis 30)

"Gideon said to God: 'Do not be angry with me for I am about to speak, but this once. I beg you to let me try this one time with the fleece. It should now be dry this once, but there should be dew on the ground.'" (Judges 6)

"[Remain there] until your brother's (Esau's) anger for you (Jacob) lessens, and he forgets what you have did to him. Then I (Rebecca) will send for you from there. Why should I be deprived of both of you in one day?" (Genesis 27)

"All your (Pharaoh's) servants shall come to me (Moses) and prostrate themselves to me, and say: 'Get out with all the people who follow you.' After that, I will go out. He then went out from Pharaoh in great anger." (Exodus 11)

"Samaria, your calf has cast you off. My anger has flared against them. How long will it be before they achieve innocence?" (Hosea 8)

"Stop acting angry and forsake wrath. Do not vex yourself as it happens only to the evil." (Psalms 37)

"Sheikh Fareed advises: Answer evil with goodness; do not fill your mind with anger. Then this body shall not suffer from any disease, and one shall obtain everything. [SGGS 1381]

"One who has an abiding faith in the holy-word, God resides within him (body and soul). He does not come or go in reincarnation, and he is rescued. Through the word of the Guru, his heart-lotus blossoms forth. Whoever is seen, is driven by hope and despair, by sexual desire, anger, corruption, hunger and thirst. Says Nanak: Those detached recluses who meet the Lord are so very rare." [SGGS 224]

"Sexual desire and anger are very powerful in the body; bless this devotee with courage and fortitude that he may rise to wage war against them, and that he may emerge victorious. Lord, please treat me as Your own and save; through the perfect Guru, drive them out. The powerful fire of corruption is raging violently within; the word of the Immaculate Guru is the icy water which soothes the body and provides solace to the mind. The mind and body are calm and tranquil; the disease has been cured, and now there's peaceful sleep. As the rays of the sun spread out everywhere, the Lord pervades each and every heart. Meeting the holy saint, one drinks in the sublime essence of the Lord; sitting in the home of the inner being, drink in the essence of His Name." [SGGS 1325]

Anger could be the consequence of an array of feelings and emotions, including victimization and betrayal, powerlessness, insecurity, failure in communication and a host of related causes. To keep the demonic force of anger, at bay, one could deploy the technique of 'stepping-back', or even think in terms of adopting a novel method of self-imposition of a penal action, for each defeat at the hands of anger.

JUDAISM & SIKHISM

Commonalities and Differences : A Synopsis

The Origins

Both started as per Divine will.
Judaism started with a communication between and the Prophet Abraham and God.
Sikhism sprang up as a revelation to Guru Nanak.
Each established a firm and distinct identity and separated themselves from the idolaters around them. From another standpoint, both claim to be revolutionary protest movements, launched to bring about a radical transformation in the psyche of the masses; both rebelled against ritualism, superstitious beliefs, prejudices and ceremonial legacies.

The Founders

As per Jewish belief, Abraham was sent to teach monotheism; God called Him 'His friend.'
As per Sikh belief, Guru Nanak was anointed through Divine Revelation, and he proclaimed himself as 'Servant of God', though he has been described by his contemporaries as 'God-incarnate'.

Divine Light

Abraham had several disciples and a large family that was charged with continuing the Divine mission.
The Divine Light, originating in Guru Nanak, was transmitted to nine successive Gurus in human-form, before finally being preserved, for eternity, in the Holy Scripture, Guru Granth Sahib.

Creation of the Universe

Both subscribe to the view that there are countless galaxies, and constellations; man cannot gauge God's extent and expansiveness.

Both religions believe that God is beyond time, space, and human comprehension, i.e.: unfathomable.
Sikhism believes that God created the entire universe with a single command; all at once, not in phases.
Judaism believes that God created everything in six days, and on the seventh day, He rested.

Idol-Worship

Both condemn it vociferously; Sikh Gurus did not seek to be venerated. Instead, the Scriptural writings are given paramount importance. Both religions disfavor idolatry (statues, symbols, icons, photographs).
In Judaism, the second of The 10 Commandments is very specific regarding this issue: You shall have no other gods before Me. You shall not make yourself a graven image, nor any manner of likeness of anything that is in heaven above or that is in the water under the earth; you shall not bow down unto them nor serve them.

Status of the Holy Congregation

In Judaism, the congregation is accorded due respect.
In Sikhism, it is designated at 'par with the Guru'.

Power of Prayer

Both believe in it. Holy congregation's prayers assume powers of healing. These prayers are heard in the Lord's court, and suffering humanity is rescued, as per God's word enshrined in the holy books.
Both believe that where there are two or more adherents, in collective prayer, there resides God.

Atonement and Repentance

Both are unanimous that righteousness, atonement and repentance, must be emphasized.
Sikhism believes "the hand that sins, suffers the punishment; all are accountable, individually". It stresses upon both, righteousness as well as repentance, in that order.

Ascetism and Celibacy

Both discourage the practice of asceticism and celibacy. The life of a householder is encouraged, as a potent vehicle for serving humanity. Also, it is considered a natural way of life, because the 'attraction' for it is unavoidable, even though a person remains a celibate; hence, the desired fruits of celibacy are not reaped.

Love and Service to Humanity

Both are vociferous in the condemnation of religious fanaticism, and conversions by deployment of force, or persuasion; it is all right if one were to embrace a religion of one's own volition, totally voluntarily.
Both believe in the dictum: "Service to humanity is service to God" and the uplifting of weaker sections of society. Both encourage the practice of 'tithe' (donating ten percent of one's honest earnings to charity).

Addictions

Both preach that all addictions/vices (adultery, prostitution, gambling, drugs, etc.) result in sin, suffering, and evil.